Stages for Tomorrow

Cover drawing

The Tricycle Theatre, in London's Kilburn High Road, was built in 1980 within the shell of a 1920s dance hall. It was so successful with actors and audiences that, following destruction by fire in 1987, it was rebuilt to the original design with only minor technical improvements.

The drawing of the Tricycle, by its architect Tim Foster, captures the essence of a format which, rediscovering the spirit of the eighteenth-century playhouse, is the core concept of many of the new theatres built in the final years of this century and most of those planned for the opening years of the next.

Stages for Tomorrow

Housing, funding and marketing live performances

Francis Reid

Focal Press

OXFORD BOSTON JOHANNESBURG MELBOURNE NEW DELHI SINGAPORE

Focal Press
An imprint of Butterworth-Heinemann
Linacre House, Jordan Hill, Oxford OX2 8DP
225 Wildwood Avenue, Woburn, MA 01801-2041
A division of Reed Educational and Professional Publishing Ltd

 A member of the Reed Elsevier plc group

First published 1998

British Library Cataloguing in Publication Data
A catalogue record for this book is available from the British Library

Library of Congress Cataloguing in Publication Data
A catalogue record for this book is available from the Library of Congress

ISBN 0 240 51515 3

Printed and bound in Great Britain by Biddles Ltd, Guildford and King's Lynn

Contents

Preface

The advent of a new century is an opportunity for taking stock. Looking back in the hope of charting a way forward. Reviewing where we have come from, considering where we are now, and attempting to identify the options ahead.

This is a book about theatre infrastructure. Its concern is not with the productions that appear on our stages but with the environment in which these performances take place. The core topic, therefore, is the architecture and management of the buildings which house performances.

Theatre is a people industry. Its plays, musicals, operas and ballets explore personal relationships. The performances pivot on the interaction of acting people and audience people. The writers, producers, directors, choreographers, designers, technicians and administrators are a creative team of people. So the infrastructure to initiate and house a live performance is based primarily on the interpersonal relationships between all the users, whether workers or audience, of a theatre building. Consequently, user friendliness is the epicentre of the debate.

After more than forty years of having a go at a wide range of jobs in the theatre, it is inevitable that this book is written from a highly personal viewpoint. Its 'thinking aloud' approach is one which will be familiar to readers of my magazine articles. Indeed they may recognise reworking of some of my earlier writings.

Throughout the twentieth century, live theatre has faced competition from a series of new technology-based media and it has survived. But as the century ends, financial pressure is close to crisis point. There is an urgent need to review the extent to which society is prepared to support live theatre through the national and local taxation systems. I hope that this book offers some small contribution to the debate.

Francis Reid

1
Performing
Live

Throughout the twentieth century, live performance has been challenged by the ever-increasing sophistication of recorded media. Nevertheless, direct contact between actor and audience has not merely survived but has flourished. Primarily, this is because live theatre generates a two-way interaction between actor and audience in the communication of ideas and emotions. Audience response ensures that no two performances of a production are ever identical. However, the survival of live performance is also a consequence of the way in which the traditional stage has been stimulated by the new art forms developed through film editing, electronic mixing and digital processing.

Survival in any area of human endeavour begins with an assessment of strengths and weaknesses. These need to be not just identified but positively acknowledged. With the advent of cinema, the weaknesses of live theatre were perhaps rather more obvious than its strengths. How could it hope to compete with a medium whose production costs could be amortised against so many seat sales? When screen first challenged stage, popular theatre was endeavouring to offer its audience a brief escape from a life of long hours of repetitive drudgery in a bleak environment. But cinema could provide escapism on an even grander scale. This was particularly important in an era when all manner of social, political and geographical horizons were opening up.

Theatre, encouraged by its audiences, had increasingly attempted to bring realistic spectacle to the stage. But, even the most sophisticated application of timber, paint, perspective and machinery was no match for the new moving pictures which could leap the barriers of location and time, offering their audience a window into a world of believable dreams. It is curious but true that the projected images of film and television can come much closer to reality than the 'real' images of the live stage. Long before the advent of the new media, and ever since, the stage has been caught between the differences of scale involved in presenting broad spectacle and subtle intimacy. Much of this dilemma is significantly reduced by the film camera's ability, unattainable in a theatre, to zoom and cut between wide panoramas and intimate close-ups. Screen close-ups may be so large that they tend to expose any lack of sincerity in the acting but, at their best, they allow the audience to see one character through another's eyes. Wide-angled panoramas may emphasise the lack of depth in the picture, but they are a vital part of the zoom capability which enables the frame to be fitted around the action. The stage, on the other hand, is under some pressure to tailor the action to fill the space.

Theatre lovers tend to be sentimental about the closure of the many stages which failed to meet the challenge of the cinema. But theatre can only exist by attracting an audience. Novelty and fashion played their part in theatre closures, as did the manner in which the lives of the newly created film stars were manipulated in pursuit of what we now call marketing. But the crucial factor, always difficult to accept, was the low quality of content and presentation which inevitably becomes an accelerating spiral of decline when audience levels fall. This was particularly evident in countries with a tradition of commercial theatre unsupported by city or state. Inability to invest not only affected production quality but also inhibited competition with the comforts of the new luxury picture palaces.

Cost differential in seat prices was an important factor in promoting cinema against theatre. But both suffered with the advent of television which, once acquired, had no significant day-to-day running costs for the viewer. There was now a strong financial incentive to stay at home where it was easier to relax, to eat, to drink and to select an alternative performance channel. Or even switch off.

The general spiral of declining quality continued in the minor theatres. Most of the actors and many of the plots in the television soaps were the same as in the closing theatres, but the standards of presentation were infinitely higher. Nationally transmitted programmes stimulated national publicity. So stars were born.

The creation of stars, first by radio and then by television, came as a life-saver to theatre. Seeing television actors, singers and comedians in the flesh became the major popular incentive for abandoning the home screen for an evening out at a live venue. This became such a crucial factor that actors were identified by their TV roles on all posters and press releases. Seeing stars live became an integral feature of the popular music industry. In the case of major recording stars, it was a promotional device whereby the costs of loss-making live appearances were recouped from increased record sales.

Today, live and recorded performances not only co-exist but feed each other.

Video tends to be strong in realism, particularly in projecting the interaction of small groups of characters, often with rapid cross-cutting between close-ups of faces. In wide views, whether landscape or corps de ballet, details can merge within the small picture area. Video is a good medium for the frenzied image manipulation which has become an indispensable feature of the visual accompaniment to pop music.

Realism is also a major strength of film which, additionally, excels at handling panoramic landscapes. This is a factor not just of screen area but also of the quality of a projected image which has more substance than the luminous picture generated within a cathode ray tube.

Some of the problems of live performance have been mentioned. What are the advantages?

Every live performance is unique. No two are identical because of performers' response to the audience reaction. This may be quite subtle although, in the case of a comedy, there can be a substantial difference in running time between a full house on a Saturday evening and a thin midweek matinee. The audience at a live performance has a sense of identity, sharing emotions, especially laughter, and responding with a more intense concentration than when the performers are but images of themselves.

A live performance has an element of danger. The possibility of something going wrong ensures that some of the opening-night tension remains in every subsequent performance of even the longest run. Audio recordings are an edited compilation of several 'takes'. The removal of fluffed notes, the rebalancing of the separate instrumental tracks and the technological marvels of digital processing can tend towards the elimination of excitement in favour of bland efficiency. Moreover, as a recording is intended to be heard over and over again, the musicians will try to give a definitive performance rather than take the interpretative risks that are common in a live concert. Apart from news and some discussion programmes, most television is now pre-recorded and subjected to a post-production process from which key members of the original production team are often excluded. Film directors are routinely excluded from an editing process which may incorporate re-editing influenced by market-oriented reactions to sneak previews. The need felt from time to time to issue a 'director's cut' of a film is significant.

Attending a live performance can induce a very strong sense of occasion. In part this is due to the trouble taken to make the decision, buy the ticket, dress up and travel. But essentially it is a response to sharing a space with a star only previously experienced on a screen, or witnessing a production only known through recordings, journalism and video excerpts. The anticipation of occasion has been increased in recent years by the way in which events are marketed and by the development of a more welcoming and anticipatory atmosphere in venues. Ever-rising cost has an influence because the fewer visits made, the more significant each becomes.

Performing live tomorrow

What does the future hold for live performance? There are strong indicators for continuing survival, not least the resilience already shown throughout a century of competing media. The major factor must surely be that live interaction with an audience is fundamental to the interpretation of drama, music and movement. To the French, the audience are those who 'assister à'. There is no limit to the technological wonders on the horizon. The reality of processed images will doubtless continue to become increasingly virtual, yet prevented from making the final transition into the natural world by the very nature of the reality which the technical media seek to emulate.

The increasing sophistication of audio visual origination, processing, recording and transmission will doubtless produce new kinds of performance. Co-existing with the more traditional forms, they will surely stimulate every aspect of the art and craft of music and drama interpretation. It does not seem unreasonable to assume that the quality of live performance will be enhanced. It will certainly survive. But whether it flourishes will depend upon the willingness to allocate sufficient resources, not just by individuals but by society as a whole.

Critics

We all get bad notices from time to time. We are human, so we twitch. We prefer good notices, not just because we are human but because we are trying to survive in a precarious profession. However, from time to time we get just a little bit annoyed by good notices because we know that on this particular occasion our work was lousy: artists must have confidence in their self-criticism. Some of us have been known to declare that we do not read notices: indeed, this is a common response from colleagues when we compliment them on receiving a favourable review. We may get depressed about bad notices in private, but try to laugh them off in public, particularly if the box office is healthy. However, if we have any sense, we shut up and we certainly do not reply to our critics. To do so might draw attention to something which very few people are likely to have read in depth, if at all.

2
Architecture

At the beginning of the twentieth century, the word 'theatre' carried clear images of a standard form of building. It was a form which had been in continuous evolution since the Renaissance, although the pace of change had been so slow and gradual that there had been apparent stability from one generation to the next. But this was the end of an era: never again would there be such standardisation of audience and stage facilities.

The twentieth-century inheritance

The twentieth century began with a large stock of relatively new theatres, most of them dating from the couple of decades spanning the turn of the century. Where theatres dated back to earlier periods, it tended to be because they had not only survived fire but were either monuments with sufficient architectural and political significance to be refurbished rather than rebuilt, or built on sites with low redevelopment potential. Central European building had tended to be a community response to a belief in the importance of culture as an integral part of national identity. Elsewhere it had been a privately-funded speculative response to a demand for entertainment.

The single-room concept of earlier theatres was lost during the nineteenth century. The stages of these theatres thrust the action into the auditorium, enhancing both visibility and audibility – plus that difficult to quantify but essential contact between actor and audience. At the start of the nineteenth century, actors had been content to play in front of, and divorced from, a scenic background. But audiences showed increasing preference for a pictorial theatre with actors and scenic environment integrated within a frame. This conflict between visual spectacle and textual nuance has been with us since the ancient theatres of Greece and Rome. It continues unresolved.

In the theatres of the late nineteenth century, there were considerable national differences in auditorium format and in the scale of audience facilities. In countries with a commercial theatre tradition, deep galleries were developed to maximise seating capacity and revenue. These theatres tended to be built on restricted sites and, although foyer spaces were often basic, architects such as Frank Matcham displayed tremendous ingenuity in exploiting small, irregularly shaped plots of land. This style of theatre was particularly evident in Britain, in its colonies, and in America.

Population centres with an earlier court theatre tradition, however, had developed a recognition of theatre as an area of civic cultural responsibility. This was particularly so in the German-speaking countries of central Europe where a tradition of court and civic subsidy allowed retention of the eighteenth-century style of shallow seating tiers which offered a more universally direct contact with the stage. These theatres were given generous conspicuous sites and a rather grand overall style which included audience circulation areas on a scale appropriate to an important public building. Initial construction and subsequent maintenance to higher standards than speculative commercial theatres has ensured a higher survival rate.

Inevitably there were reactions to the standard proscenium theatre with its circles and boxes. A particularly strong and influential reaction was that of Richard Wagner who, seeking a more integrated total fusion of text, music, acting and scenic environment, looked afresh at the auditorium of the classic theatre of the Greeks and Romans. Boxes and balconies were discarded in favour of a single rising fan-shaped tier offering all members of the audience a clear sightline to a picture stage. The proscenium was still present but less positively defined as a frame. Wagner's Bayreuth Festspielhaus was to be a major influence on subsequent theatre design.

But in general, by the beginning of the twentieth century, 'theatre' had become synonymous with a proscenium framed stage offering, to an audience stacked on every available wall surface of the auditorium, a window into a world of illusion.

Twentieth-century developments

An art century rarely coincides with the neat chronology of one hundred years. The twentieth century for theatre architecture effectively runs from the end of the First World War until the eruption of democracy across eastern Europe, from the dominance of cinema through the stay-at-home of television to the time shift flexibility of video recorders.

For much of the twentieth century, theatre-building designers tended to react against the past, rejecting the good equally with the bad. During the final decade or so, rediscovery has been the predominant influence. Reassessment of fundamentals has led to redeployment of solutions which had been slowly evolved but hastily discarded. The results are far from pastiche.

The danger is that in rediscovering the past we may once again reject what is good in the present. Twentieth-century theatre architecture was notable for its indiscriminate reaction against the past. In the main, theatre buildings, certainly those inherited from the nineteenth century and before, are now regarded as heritage only to be redeveloped after debate. But this is a recent trend: as twentieth-century theatre building got underway, the existing theatres were seen as something to be reacted against in a search for the new.

Economics, social change, technological development, war, and the emergence of new media tend to be the prime factors in theatrical development.

The cinema, inevitably, was the major influence when theatre building got underway again after the First World War. Clear straight-ahead lines of sight to the stage from all seats in the house became the prime architectural virtue. This stemmed from the technical requirements of viewing two-dimensional projected images on a screen. Most new theatres, if not specifically intended for mixed-media operation as cine-variety, certainly intended to hedge their bets by incorporating picture-house capability.

But, technology apart, there was a pressing need for theatres to respond to the challenge of the cinema. It was virtually impossible to compete with the glamour and excitement of the new medium with its stars, exotic locations and mega-budgets, but new theatres could copy the cinema's improved standards of audience comfort. The old theatres certainly had some comfortable seats but there was a rigid hierarchy extending from luxury, through declining degrees of comfort, to a level of discomfort that tested the dedication of the audience. And these various parts of the house tended to be rigidly segregated with separate access through dedicated entrances.

The war had triggered a rapidly changing social climate to which the cinema responded. Thrown into a topsy-turvy situation with the worst and therefore cheapest seats now being these nearest to the stage, it was natural for the cinema to aim for equal standards of comfort in all parts of a house approached by a single entrance.

Considerable new thinking about the whole nature of theatre focused on the relationship between actor and audience. There was also an increasingly perceptible shift from the standard turn-of-the-century view of theatre as just a place of entertainment towards what the Danes had long enshrined in the wording above the proscenium arch of their National Theatre in Copenhagen: Ei Blot Til Lyst – not for entertainment only. There was nothing new in this concept. Central Europe had always placed more emphasis upon culture and it was from there that the idea of theatre as art spread outwards. Indeed Wagner's dedication to the *gesamkunst* (complete art) ideal of integrated ideas, words, music and images had inspired the fan-shaped auditorium which was the basic shape of the movie theatre.

Outside Italy, the late nineteenth century had seen boxes, once uniform and continuous around the galleries, decrease in number but increase in grandeur, concentrating around the proscenium as a positive feature of the imposing frame. Now they became residual, often to the point of being purely decorative and not seriously intended for viewing the stage. Whereas at least three audience tiers had been common, a desire to reduce extreme vertical sightlines made a single balcony normal. With boxes removed and balconies no longer curving around the sides of the auditorium, walls became decorative surfaces rather than a place to hang people. Providing every member of the audience with a clear sightline in this way resulted in the furthest seats being a longer distance from the stage than they would be in a traditional theatre with a similar proscenium opening and seating capacity.

Broadway theatres brought large audiences close to the actors by opting for very wide stages – fine for musicals but less satisfactory for drama. Even so, any house of considerable size had problems of viewing distance from its back rows, a problem increased at ground level by the tunnelling effect of balcony overhang. The large screen images of cinema gave the view from the distant rows an acceptable scale, but with live theatre the effect was that of looking through a reversed telescope.

Shallow balconies extending all around the auditorium persisted in central Europe where much theatre was in the operatic tradition. Elsewhere the walls where the audience had once hung were now devoted to Art Deco. The exotic fibrous plaster impressions of Arabia, India and the Far East which Matcham had used at the turn of the century to offer exotic fantasies on a suburban night out were now the province of many cinemas. Theatres tended to follow the alternative movie-house style of clean lines, soft curves and concealed cove lighting.

In all periods there are small pockets of experiment which buck the general trend. Accounting for a minimal proportion of the total theatre activity, they are the seeds of future mainstream development. The period between the wars was particularly active in this respect and much of the thinking that was to influence new directions in staging modes during the rest of the century had its roots in these experiments, many of which were particularly concerned with discarding the proscenium arch. German experiments with non-naturalistic staging were developing new forms of theatre experience which had strong repercussions for architectural form, and this trend was accelerated by the dispersal of Nazi exiles across Europe and America.

The war years

Between 1939 and 1945, the world stock of theatres decreased. The aeroplane carried war to most cities of Europe and many theatres were destroyed or damaged beyond immediate repair. In countries at war but beyond the area of conflict, the economics and philosophies at a time of war precluded new theatre construction. In countries not involved in the conflict, the uncertainties of war made theatre building seem a somewhat frivolous use of resources.

The German opera houses remained open until 1944, often with patched-up bomb damage, and key festivals remained in operation – Bayreuth until 1943 and Salzburg without interruption. The painted panels and baroque plasterwork of Munich's 1753 Cuvilliestheater were dismantled for safe storage in 1943. So, although the theatre, operating with temporary fittings, was destroyed by bombing six weeks later, a reconstruction was possible in 1958. Aleoti's Parma Theatre of 1619 was less fortunate, although comparison of pictures of the destruction with those of the reconstructed theatre show just what can be achieved when there is a total building record available in plans and photographs. Indeed the replacement of lost sections in plain wood without any attempt at replicating the decoration somehow even seems to have enhanced authenticity.

In Britain, the ailing touring theatre chains had a reprieve from decline with a surge of audience, many geographically displaced by the conditions of war, in search of entertainment. The repertory theatres flourished despite casting difficulties caused by conscription. In general there was a hunger for music, ballet and serious theatre. This was supported and stimulated by CEMA (Council for Encouragement of Music and the Arts), the forerunner of the Arts Council. Britain was on the way, for the first time, to having national support for the arts through an agency funded by central government. Building construction or even maintenance could not be a feature of this arts activity but the excitement generated in discussions about post-war reconstruction laid down the basics on which much of the new theatre building of the second half of the century would be undertaken.

The most vocal theatre lobby among the arts came from supporters of drama. The provincial repertory theatres had established a pre-war toehold and this was consolidated as a foothold during the war years. This was not true repertory with a repertoire of several productions alternating in a nightly sequence. Only one production was performed at a time, for a short run – usually with a weekly change and known as 'weekly rep'. In many cases the theatres were small and converted from halls, corn exchanges and the like. These were the serious playhouses, consciously seeking a theatre more concerned with stimulating the mind than providing the relaxing entertainment which was the province of commercial rep – also weekly but playing twice nightly. The achievements of rep theatres, playing eight or twelve performances in a week while rehearsing another play in the same period, strains today's imagination, even of those who were present.

The rep lobby looked towards a regional grid of producing companies, each in their purpose-built modern playhouse. Their wish was to be gradually fulfilled before the end of the century. Supporters of lyric theatre – opera, dance and the musical – were not vocal on a regional scale. Their ambitions were focused on establishing national companies by consolidating groups which had hitherto existed on an *ad hoc* basis.

Post-war reconstruction

The most remarkable feature of the immediate post-war period was the speed with which defeated European cities reopened their theatres. Even in the most devastated industrial towns of Germany, the civic cultural tradition gave resumption of performances as high a priority as all the other essential services. Where buildings were damaged beyond temporary patching, interim theatres were hastily contrived. The companies, particularly the opera companies, had survived and they soon found somewhere to perform. For example, the auditorium of the Hamburg Staatsoper had burned out but the backstage area was saved by the fire curtain. The original stage was sufficiently large to accommodate an interim stage, orchestra pit and auditorium. The rear elevators were raised to form a stage level, the next lowered to form a pit and the remainder staggered to give good sightlines from 600 seats. Auditorium walls were formed with scenery while chandeliers from *Der Rosenkavalier* provided light and token elegance. As the German economic miracle got under way in the 1950s there was an intensive programme of theatre construction which was a major influence on the design of new theatres everywhere. A feature of these new theatres was massive stage areas with complex technology to allow large-scale productions to play in repertoire. This involves not just a nightly permutation from a large selection of current productions but also scenery changeovers each afternoon from morning rehearsals of new additions to the repertoire.

In Britain the touring theatre chains which had enjoyed a temporary wartime revival now entered into a spiral of decline which accelerated as television coverage expanded to cover the country. The addition of an independent network brought a competition for viewers in which the newcomers forced the hitherto staid BBC to join it in scheduling programmes with a more positive slant towards entertainment.

Touring theatres in smaller towns (known as the Number Twos and Threes) responded with a desperate descent into revues with suggestive titles, featuring nudes presented in the static poses permitted by the laws of the time. The downward spiral accelerated towards widespread closures. The buildings, long starved of investment, were now bleak, frayed and inhospitable – a long way from the escapist palaces of their origin. Many were converted to shops or their sites lost to development. A few survived as bingo halls, providing a heritage for which we would be grateful a few decades later. The larger 'Number Ones' survived with fragile commercial viability for a little longer – basically on a diet of mixed entertainment with Christmas pantomime providing a major annual boost, keeping a home available for occasional opera and ballet tours.

But with regional playhouses, Britain now entered into a theatre-building boom with a zeal comparable to that of the Georgians and Victorians in their eras of expansion. With the cities which had thriving reps in improvised premises taking the lead, communities of all sizes began to consider the possibility of their own rep. For the first time Britain joined central Europe in regarding a civic theatre, not commercially operated, as a desirable public amenity. The 'me too' of civic pride can be a very powerful motivator. But it was fortunate that British aspirations, or at least the aspirations of its most powerful lobbyists, were directed towards building and running small playhouses rather than large lyric theatres. Such aspirations could just about be matched to the resources available, or at least to the scale of resourcing that could be conceived as possible.

The new buildings were democratic in concept, with clear sightlines from all seats plus good audience amenities and catering facilities. Encouraged by the strong regular theatregoer aspects of the membership clubs and play-goer societies of what had become known as 'The Repertory Movement', these theatres were seen as facilities to be open all day rather than just half an hour before curtain-up. They were planned as comprehensive drama factories with full production manufacturing facilities for scenery and costumes located within the building.

The new theatres of Britain were proudly functional. Decorative elements were an unacceptable frivolity. This was not just a matter of modernist building style, it was a manifestation of serious purpose. The 1956 (and 1965) London visits of Brecht's Berliner Ensemble had rallied the protagonists of theatre as a serious political and social force dealing with mankind's agonies rather than with the potential civilising influences of beautiful sights, sounds and thoughts. Concrete was the medium, fair faced or shuttered. Paint was shunned unless it was black.

In the United States, much of the new theatre construction in the immediate post-war decades took place on the campus. The universities expanded their already established drama departments and many played a crucial role in developing regional theatre through acting companies associated with them and playing in their theatres. A series of large campus touring theatres augmented the traditional 'road' touring houses of the cities. With a strictly commercial approach to funding (although with tax legislation encouraging individual and corporate sponsorship generosity) there was an emphasis on large buildings to maximise seating capacity. With a democratic insistence on purity of sightline from all seats, some of these theatres were very large indeed.

With the exception of Germany and Italy, where a strong opera house tradition prevailed, the unifying international feature was a clear sightline to the stage from a house which had its roots in Bayreuth and the cinema, its walls and ceiling increasingly modelled to accommodate the requirements of lighting technology.

15

The aspect of theatre form most agonised over in the immediate post-war decades was the proscenium arch. Indeed the alleged communication barrier of the proscenium frame was a subject to induce a polemic response from the otherwise most rational of theatre pundits. There seemed to be something of a consensus view that a theatre should be a single room – not an acting room joined to an audience room and viewed through a proscenium window. The actor/audience relationship was at the heart of theatre experience and any hint of physical separation was a threat. While there was general agreement that the actor/audience contact was critical, how to achieve it was the subject of heated debate. Did the proscenium actually stand in the way? And if so, to what extent should the stage thrust – or should it be surrounded by audience?

Temporary thrust stages built in old theatres were very successful for audience at ground level in the stalls, but mostly offered hopeless sightlines for anyone upstairs other than those in the front rows of balconies. When thrust stages were incorporated into new proscenium theatres with pure sightlines, the sense of thrust was only felt close to the stage. From most seats the effect was that of an end stage. And indeed the end stage, with no thrust but no proscenium, provided a very successful popular single-room theatre. Elidir Davies's conversion of a Thames warehouse at Puddle Dock for Bernard Miles – the Mermaid – became a reference with a seminal effect on many subsequent theatres.

Probably the most influential result of the proscenium debate was the design of theatres to place as little emphasis on the proscenium opening as possible. Hitherto, theatres had tended to make a feature of the proscenium. Some Victorian theatres even structured it like a gilded picture frame and between-the-wars theatres often used Art Deco columns or complex plaster coving incorporating soft decorative lighting. Now the aim was to stress the proscenium as little as possible. The stage started at the natural termination of the auditorium walls, the ceiling sloping down and the walls curving in.

The seminal thrust stage was that devised by Tyrone Guthrie for the 1948 Edinburgh Festival revival of the 1542 *Ain Satyre of the Thrie Estaites* in the Church of Scotland Assembly Hall. Raked seating on three sides at floor and gallery levels focused on to a highish thrust stage whose sides were formed from continuous stepping which allowed entrances to be made down any of the auditorium aisles and onto the stage. A gallery at the rear could be used for scenic elements, musicians, etc. Such a stage, being temporary, could be given varying formats from festival to festival and over the years has turned out to be very versatile.

A comparison of early thrust theatres reveals experiments with the basic design problems, particularly stage height and auditorium rake. The need to build over fixed furnishings kept the Edinburgh stage high. Chichester's initial small rise was soon increased. Some subsequent thrust stages have used floor level as the stage. Sheffield was given a flexible stage with a perimeter which could become a moat, provide entrances from below or become a pit for musicians. In some theatres, such as Leeds Playhouse, the thrust was restricted and the audience were seated in an arc which did not fully extend around the sides of the stage.

Thrust stages exercised such a power on the thinking of the time that minimal provision was made in all new theatres: it became standard to have an elevator in front of the stage which could carry extra seats at floor level, sink to form an orchestra pit or rise to form an apron which, although often labelled thrust, was a very token thrust indeed.

German civic theatres in the medium-sized cities play a repertoire which includes opera, operetta, dance and drama. To house simultaneous performances they usually incorporate two auditoria: a Grosses Haus and a Kleines Haus. These are normally, but not rigidly, dedicated to opera and drama – a big play may occupy some nights on the big stage while an experimental musical is on the little one. The Kleines Haus became a flexible room where various thrust options were possible.

Total flexibility seemed so desirable that 'Adaptable Theatres' was the most common phrase in articles, lectures, debates and conferences. There were attempts to achieve this by machinery, particularly in America. A number of theatres were devised with a modular floor which could have sections raised or lowered, often using complex hydraulics, to position stage and audience in any configuration. But these mechanised theatres were found to be particularly limiting. The most flexible space is the empty room in which any desired theatre can be constructed. However, this requires lots of labour and time. And indeed a feature of the adaptable theatres of this period was that however they were designed – and some quite innovative possibilities of bleacher seating were devised – they usually settled down very quickly into being used in what was found to be their most satisfactory format. This was often end stage.

Theatre-in-the-round was promoted with missionary fervour in post-war Britain by Stephen Joseph and two such major permanent theatres may be traced directly to his influence. Mostly, however, the totally surrounded stage tends to be seen as one of the options in a flexible studio-type environment where it allows a relatively large number of audience to be particularly close to the stage. The Royal Exchange in Manchester, a self-contained module built on the old cotton trading floor, has glazed walls and does not try to be a completely dark room or to dissociate itself from the building in which it has been placed. High shallow galleries surround a centre acting area. These experimental theatres co-existed with the more conventional houses and were a considerable influence on the next generation of theatres to evolve.

A brief moment of standardisation

By the late 1960s a standard form, or series of forms, was emerging – although many of the 1960s designs were not built until well into the 1970s and even, in some cases, the 1980s. This was a period when there was almost a consensus as to what was meant by a new theatre. Its concrete exterior was almost certainly uncompromisingly functional. Despite the best intentions of planning authorities who sought to restrict or disguise the height of fly towers, many of the better-looking theatres made a feature of functional necessity and let the fly tower proclaim the nature of the building it crowned. Geometric modules were a favourite starting point with curves, as in Düsseldorf's Schauspielhaus, quite rare. Alas, angular geometry could lead to operational problems by inserting backstage oblique walls where clear rectangular space is desirable.

Large, often luxurious, audience-circulation areas had glass outer walls so that the theatres looked enticingly come hither when lit up at night – although there were those who believed that such emphasis on the social aspects could discourage potential audiences from the idea of theatregoing.

Ceilings and walls were designed around production lighting require-ments. People no longer papered side walls, except in the German-speak-ing countries which continued their tradition of shallow boxes and circles but now angled them to face the stage to improve sightlines. Some theatres, particularly in central Europe, had restrained decoration, even gilding. But the favoured interior style tended to involve single saturated colours for car-pets and seating, with strong directional downlighting to remove emphasis from side walls which were often untreated concrete.

In Britain there were lots of playhouses with around 500 seats, in central Europe many opera houses had just over 1000, and in America they just seemed to get bigger and bigger with well over 2000 as a normal starting point.

German opera houses had their associated smaller theatres, usually flexible in format, and it gradually became customary to include a small studio within a British rep building.

In the Sydney Opera House, Australia gave the century one of its great architectural monuments and the only new theatre to be instantly recognis-able to everyone around the world irrespective of whether they ever visited one.

Although not completed until the mid-1970s, the National Theatre on London's South Bank summarised many of the trends of the 1960s. Its two main auditoria were in much of the spirit of the regional reps. The Lyttle-ton is a proscenium house and remains firmly so, despite elaborate arrange-ments for tinkering with the proscenium zone. The Olivier represents an attempt at the open-stage single-room philosophy with its stage thrusting into a sharply rising arc of seating. For budgeting reasons, the smaller Cottesloe auditorium was disguised as a void during much of the design and building periods. This allowed it to incorporate more up-to-date think-ing than was possible within the concept-to-opening time-scale of the main houses. It was also subject to much less committee compromise. Thus, while firmly in the black box studio tradition, the Cottesloe incorporated the courtyard galleries that are central to the major rethink in theatre philo-sophy that was already underway and would soon accelerate.

Two features of the problems of mounting central European-style operations without central European levels of financial resourcing were confirmed. Comprehensive workshops place construction under the theatre's immediate control but the inevitable difficulties in programming work flow tend to make the cost more than using outside contractors. And true repertoire is costly in actor salaries and technical changeovers.

A major success was the way in which the National Theatre adopted and developed the growing policy of using a theatre's foyers as an open-all-day meeting place. To do otherwise is now considered unthinkable.

Back to basics

It was inevitable that the growth in the size and complexity of theatres would provoke a reaction. 'Let's get back to basics.' 'Two planks and a passion is all that is needed to stage a dramatic event.' 'Theatre does not need hierarchical organisations and monumental buildings.'

'Fringe' and 'alternative' are perhaps the words most associated with this movement which became particularly strong during the 1970s. While much of it did make political or social comment, its anarchy was more particularly a response to the structured formalities – even solemnities – of mainstream theatre. It set out to be cheap and cheerful, utilising available spaces, improvising a performance environment without the aid of any but the most primitive technologies. Its performances mixed words, dance and music with a disregard for what was seen as the ponderous logic of the established playhouses.

A street corner or a couple of planks are a fine place to project a passion, but if that passion is projected with any success it will soon attract an audience who will require seating arranged so that they can see the actors. It will be necessary to devise a means of getting them to these seats, not forgetting taking their money. Success will require raising the planks so that more people can see. Where will the actors dress? Toilets and refreshments? In no time at all we have invented a theatre building.

In Britain the fringe was, and remains, mainly a touring operation with productions kept small for mounting in a wide range of spaces. The result has been that many spaces not originally thought of as theatres have had staging facilities added – particularly scaffolding lighting rigs. Arts Centres include basic performing spaces as part of their facilities and, all over the world, interesting buildings have been turned into simple theatres. There is virtually no space which cannot be adapted for performance.

Looking back to move forward

During the 1970s, there was a gradual realisation that something of the excitement of the old theatres had been lost. There had been so much emphasis upon the relationship between actor and audience that the other fundamental relationship of performance had been overlooked – the inter-action between members of an audience that makes them more than just an assembly of individuals. This was largely the result of rigorously pursuing the ideal of perfect sightlines to the stage. Having a pure sightline can be like sitting in isolation, whereas in the older theatres each member of the audience was aware of their fellows.

The principle of papering side walls with people had never been entirely lost in Germany where most of the post-war opera houses had a series of boxes angled towards the stage or continued their shallow balconies along the side walls, often with just a single row of seats. Either method tended to stop well before the orchestra pit to allow space for spotlight slots and for flexible proscenium structures.

So once again audience began to be hung on the walls. Galleries or boxes returned to the side wall in a movement that gathered force in Britain and quickly spread to Canada and the United States.

Initially the smaller houses tended towards a rectangular format rather than the curved horseshoes or bells of the traditional theatre. The wrap-around galleries on at least two levels were shallow and tended to be a single row of seats with perhaps two at the lowest level. In the playhouses, if not in the bigger lyric theatres, even the centre sections of the galleries remained relatively shallow and free from cantilevered overhang in the Victorian tradition. Indeed the entire auditorium tended to be contained within a room in the Georgian manner.

In their smaller versions, the courtyard theatres lent themselves very well to a promenade style of production where the action moves around the auditorium with the audience making way for the performers as the acting area ebbs and flows. In some theatres such as the National Theatre's Cottesloe where promenade productions are particularly successful, this is aided by connecting the galleries with wide, open stairways behind the seating. However, for other production styles there is much in favour of a wall immediately behind the seats to confine the space and focus audience attention.

The rectangular linearity of the first courtyard theatres was partly a consequence of the geometric functionalism of the post-war era and partly of the spaces (often found spaces in existing buildings) in which the theatres were constructed. But further looking backward to find a way forward produced more curves, and even the addition of non-functional decorative elements.

Hanging people on walls is not an ideal situation. Sightlines get progressively worse as seats are placed higher and closer to the stage. In the old theatres people sat in boxes for social reasons – to be seen rather than to see – and seats could be highly priced accordingly. Today such seats are the cheapest in the house – indeed it is in the interest of a good performance to sell them cheaply enough to ensure that they will be filled to help the house gel. For the poorer seats in any theatre, the basic alternatives are pure sightline and long-distance lack of contact with the stage or impaired sightline and close contact. People-papered walls get more people closer to the stage.

The courtyard 'rediscovery' [as the movement became labelled] has been perhaps the major influence in the final decades of the century. Most new theatres of this period are either built in this format or show increasing concern with minimising isolation and emphasising contact between individual audience members. Theatre complexes with more than one auditorium have increasingly included a 'courtyard'. For example, the 1990 West Yorkshire Playhouse has both thrust and courtyard auditoria, enabling productions to be mounted in a wide range of styles.

The quest for adaptability

Throughout the second half of the twentieth century there has been much talk of an adaptable theatre. Many solutions have been proposed and some have been tried. The best results have been in small studio theatres, but even there the tendency has been to settle down into the most successful format. Some have limited adaptability with just two or three basic formats: but even with this, the degree of compromise has to be such that neither is ideal. There have been lots of complex versions of the proscenium zone, but essentially these have just been tinkerings with the framing of one stage form: they have had little significance for the actor/audience relationship beyond the first few rows.

The adaptability problem is not just one of being able to change format for today's productions. Performance ideals and staging methods develop over the life of a theatre building and current construction materials are particularly intransigent when it comes to future structural modifications. The pouring of concrete imposes current decisions on future generations.

This was not a problem for earlier theatres. There was a permanent shell of stone and brick but it was fitted out internally with a timber structure which was virtually free standing. During the seventeenth, eighteenth and early nineteenth centuries in particular, developments in auditorium format were carried out by the stage carpenters and scenic artists. A return to this adaptability at last seems possible. New technology, in the form of the air castor, permits large sections of stage and auditorium to be moved around, floating on a cushion of compressed air on the hovercraft principle. The particular advantages are that heavy units can be moved with very little manpower, but once the air supply to the castor has been switched off the units sit on the floor as solidly as if they were permanent. The viability has been demonstrated by such theatres as Derngate in Northampton and Cerritos in California.

Architecture tomorrow

As we move towards an increasingly leisured society, what sort of performances will we be building venues for? Is there any accord, any grand consensus between performers, the cultural establishment, funding bodies and audience? Or are they all exhausted by the strain of short-term financing in a world where Development Director has become the job title for the person in charge of raising money to survive?

Immediate consideration of current politics and funding apart, how can we plan our venues for the future? Without resorting to a crystal ball, we cannot hope to predict very far ahead. So the only realistic option is to plan for what can be foreseen, taking care that our buildings are as flexible as possible. In practice this may mean ensuring, primarily, that we do not include, as permanent, such features as may just be a passing whim or too much of a peccadillo of client, consultant or architect.

Can there ever be a truly adaptable theatre building, even with new technology? Or will there be several co-existing forms? Large communities may be able to justify complexes which include venues of various size and format, but smaller towns are almost certainly going to demand considerable adaptability.

What are the options? And the limitations? The maximum and minimum are relatively straightforward to identify but the optimum is elusive – a building that will fulfil its present requirement yet be sympathetic to changing needs in the future? Pragmatism is unavoidable but the inevitable compromises for each particular venue must result from an informed debate.

Which alternative forms can we currently envisage being required in future? Can these forms be categorised? Or do they merge too gradually into each other? The possible variations certainly can be very subtle but there are broad options within which the design of any particular venue may be approached. The major options are type of performance, mode of operation and format of stage/auditorium.

Performance types

- *Drama* demanding close contact between actor and audience, allowing subtleties of facial movement to be visible, with an acoustic favourable to speech clarity.

- *Lyric* requiring contact more in the nature of rapport than physical proximity so that an opera singer's facial mechanics of vocal production do not intrude, and the choreographic images of ballet, whether soloists or large corps of dancers, can be encompassed within the field of vision. This visual width needs to matched by an aural range to encompass a wide dynamic and provide a degree of reverberation to enhance the timbre of vocal and instrumental sounds.

- *Concert* where simple formalised visual presentation places emphasis on the quality of natural sound.

- *Spectacle* embracing high-technology musicals and solo appearances of recording stars with an emphasis on broad visual effect and on electronically processed sound which aspires to the style, quality and volume of the best hi-fi CD player or personal stereo.

Operational modes

- *Producing venues* manufacture their own product and therefore require comprehensive rehearsal, workshop, storage, and office facilities.

- *Repertoire venues* prepare and perform a series of productions in an alternating daily sequence. In this case, space and equipment is required to facilitate a quick turnround of productions.

- *Receiving theatres* perform production packages which have been prepared in producing theatres. Although they require less manufacturing space, they do need facilities for maintaining and repairing the physical aspects of touring productions. For maximum flexibility in adapting to a wide range of production styles, receiving stages need to be spacious and unencumbered by equipment associated with specialised staging methods. This space requirement is particularly necessary in receiving theatres visited by touring opera and dance companies which play in repertoire.

- *Theatres for runs*, whether the open-ended run-for-ever optimism of the West End and Broadway or the new houses being built around the world for international spectacular musicals, can be more basic in their backstage arrangements.

Stage/auditorium format

The heart of a theatre's format is the relationship between the stage and the auditorium. Within this relationship, the core of an auditorium design will be the way in which it approaches the relationship of the audience members one to another, while much of the stage design will be a response to technical factors. The relationship between stage and auditorium has a range of variation that seems to approach the infinite. Nevertheless there would seem to be eight identifiable points around which these variations are based:

- *Proscenium* The interface between auditorium and stage is clearly defined by a proscenium with many variations from an unstressed termination of walls and ceiling to a formalised frame.

- *End stage* The stage shares the same room as the auditorium but is at one end. Essentially a proscenium theatre without a proscenium.

- *Courtyard* The stage is at one end, probably but not necessarily without any conscious framing other than the termination of very shallow balconies which run all around the walls at more than one level.

- *Thrust* The stage thrusts into the seating area so that the audience are within an arc of about 90–120 degrees.

- *Deep thrust* The extent of the thrust is increased so that the audience is grouped on three sides – i.e. within an arc of 180 degrees.

- *Traverse*   The stage runs through the auditorium, so that there is an audience on two sides with actor access from both ends.

- *Surrounded*   A theatre-in-the-round may be of any geometric shape but the acting area is surrounded by audience. Actor access is through the audience by aisles and/or vomitoria, and possibly, though occasionally, through traps in the stage floor.

- *Promenade*   The ultimate single-room theatre where neither stage nor auditorium are permanently defined. The acting area shifts to various points and the audience moves to make way for the action.

Compatibility between forms

To what extent are all the variations of type, operation and format mutually exclusive? How far can the differences be compromised?

Mode of operation

A theatre designed for producing its own shows will be able to receive outside productions easily. However, a theatre with only facilities to receive will have difficulties in attempting to produce shows. Yet the provision of production facilities is difficult to justify on financial grounds unless they are going to be used intensively. Generosity may provide building capital but is unlikely to extend to running costs. Similarly, it is easy to have a run of a single production in a theatre designed for repertoire, but very difficult to play rep without the appropriate facilities. There are many cases of theatres operating successfully under just such difficulties – even producing a repertoire in houses designed for receiving runs – but the wastage in money and personal effort can be horrendous.

Types of performance

The differences between spoken drama and musical theatre are virtually incompatible. Some musicals are small and intimate. Some plays can be staged with a broad epic sweep. But in terms of intimacy and acoustic, a good lyric theatre is a poor house for drama. Conversely, unless a musical work is quite small – perhaps a play incorporating songs, or an eighteenth-century opera originally written for the resources of a small court theatre – the volume of the auditorium in a theatre of playhouse scale is insufficient to contain the sound. While many contemporary dance works are written for an intimate theatre, the great classical ballets not only need big stages but can have their overall impact lessened by being viewed too closely. Differences between musicals and spectaculars are less distinct. The spectacle house will be bigger: its stage to hold the technology of performance and its auditorium to hold the necessary box-office income. Indeed there is no clear dividing line as to when a lyric theatre becomes a house for spectaculars. Certainly the division is not so much a matter of size but of acoustic: a lyric theatre will be able to perform the large opera and dance repertoire with natural sound, whereas a spectacle house, although capable of an occasional *Aida* or so, is likely to be not just dependent upon sound reinforcement but will be geared to a sound which is intended to be electronically processed.

Formats

In many respects the prosceniuum stage is the most flexible. Certainly to the extent that the alternative forms tend to be so individual in size, shape and character that they can only accept productions which have been planned especially to suit their features. This makes the proscenium stage the most suitable one for touring. It is also the format which can most readily handle lyric theatre. Opera and dance works almost need to be specially written for alternative stage forms and, unless on a small scale, can have sound-balancing problems. The conventional pit of the proscenium theatre is the only satisfactory way to handle the large opera orchestra. Placing the orchestra in acoustic isolation elsewhere in the building, or even in another building, and conveying the sound electronically may be acceptable for a musical composed with this intent but is not suitable for the standard opera repertoire.

End stages have a similar flexibility in receiving shows, although for the bigger shows the proscenium brings many organisational benefits, particularly in relation to managing fire risks. The big proscenium stages are suitable for spectaculars and many, particularly in the popular music field, are geared to adapting to concert hall platforms. The larger lyric proscenium theatres are often used as concert halls – using an acoustic shell to focus the sound towards the auditorium rather than let it be dissipated through the technical areas surrounding the stage.

Various degrees of thrust provide a possible concert format but there tends to be considerable differences in size and acoustic between the drama and concert requirement.

Flexibility

Consequently, the flexibility in terms of operational mode and performance-type of the various formats may be summarised in broad terms as:

- *Proscenium* The traditional proscenium theatre, providing it has an unstressed frame, provides the most flexible stage for receiving a wide range of touring productions. It is suitable for the larger lyric works, particularly the great classical operas and ballets. It can be used, subject to acoustic design, for concerts and, dependent upon size, for the more spectacular areas of production. Only the smaller proscenium theatres are really suitable for drama.

- *End stage* The point where a proscenium stage becomes an end stage is not sharply defined and so in most cases it will meet the same usage areas as proscenium, subject to size. However, in larger theatres some form of proscenium makes the complexities of technology easier to handle.

- *Thrust and deep thrust* The more a stage thrusts into the auditorium, the more that theatre tends to have an individuality to which any touring company has to adapt. Many smaller fringe companies adopt a production style which

29

makes it possible for them to make rapid adjustments to accommodate a wide range of formats. But as the size and formality of a company increases, particularly the complexity of its scenery, such adaptations become difficult. However, concerts can generally adapt to a thrusting stage – subject to a suitable acoustic.

- *Traverse and In-the-round* These are really rather individual and require quite a lot of re-spacing of touring productions – even for the most flexibly minded fringe companies.

- *Promenade* Promenade productions can take place with varying success in most formats, with the various forms of single room being more sympathetic and the courtyard being perhaps the best.

- *Courtyard* Like the proscenium and end stages to which it is related – particularly the earlier theatres built for contact rather than sight – the courtyard is perhaps the most flexible and can be built in all sizes from studio to opera house.

Multi-function

A large population centre may have the resources to support, and the audience to fill, several theatres, each dedicated to the needs of specific areas of the performing arts. But how can a wide range of performance types be housed in communities which because of low population density or other resource restrictions are unable, or perhaps unwilling, to build on such a scale?

The difficulties of compromise between various theatre forms has been noted. The capital building and running resource of any producing facility is on such a scale as to require justification by a very positive commitment to produce (that is, to manufacture productions in every physical and creative sense). But what are the limitations of flexibility in relation to the scale, form and relationship of the acting and audience areas (which are essentially independent of the producing/receiving option)? Should we build very positively in one format, with flexibility so limited that there will be negligible compromise of that format? Or should we accept some limited compromise in order to provide limited flexibility?

New technology has increased the possibility of the long-desired multi-form theatre. Is the capital cost justified? Or the running costs of maintaining the technological equipment and staffing the changeovers? Is the future a mix of alternative forms with very limited variations? Or total multi-form flexibility? Or a mix of the two modes? The decision will ultimately depend upon the finance required to build, maintain and utilise the various degrees of flexible space.

The brief

The brief is, by definition, crucial to any design process. For a theatre its preparation is particularly tricky. In many cases any shortcomings in a building's fulfilment of its required functions can be traced directly to a lack of an initial clear consensus as to that theatre's intended purpose.

There are lots of decisions to be made. Who will make them? The client has the responsibility. But is the client aware of all the options? Has the architect ever built a theatre before? Many planning decisions are heavily influenced by the client's artistic director and technical personnel. But they have often changed by opening night: theatre people are basically transients while theatres not only take a long time to plan and build but, in a concrete age, even longer to alter. Clearly, there is a need for independent advice. Consequently it has become increasingly common practice to seek independent consultative advice to stimulate debate on all decision areas by ensuring that the client is aware of all available options and their implications. Feasibility studies initiate discussions to establish proposals and assess their viability. This process is helpful not only in establishing the best kind of theatre in cases where there is uncertainty, but also in testing the validity of the claims of any lobby group who have formulated positive ideas.

As the twentieth century opened there may have been a clearly established idea of a theatre building but as the century closes, the future of performance architecture lies in a series of co-existing forms. Henceforward, anyone commissioning a building to stage live performances will have to establish precisely what is required today, but attempt to omit obstacles which might inhibit performances in an unknown tomorrow.

A check list

When I approach a new theatre for the first time, the questions running through my head include:

- Will the outside achieve the right mix of dignity and come hither?

- Will the foyers welcome and impress, yet still allow a moment of excitement – a tingle of expectancy – on crossing the threshold into the auditorium?

- Will the auditorium seem smaller than its seating capacity suggests?

- Will the decorative treatment of the auditorium succeed in balancing assembly splendour with performance neutrality?

- Will the auditorium lighting combine a welcoming brightness with a subtle chiaroscuro?

- Will the proscenium zone be equally convincing in all its arrangements?

- Will the overall approach avoid the functionally bland, and err on the side of honest theatrical vulgarity rather than discrete good taste?

Consultants

The profession of theatre consultant evolved naturally out of that of lighting designer. With the rapid expansion of lighting technology in the early 1960s, lighting designers were asked to advise on the provision of spotlight mounting positions. While looking at plans, it was natural for them to be invited to comment on other aspects – or for them to volunteer advice when they spotted some simple but obvious deficiency such as the absence of access for scenery. This wider consultancy role came easily to lighting designers because of the nature of their profession which demands considerable articulacy and diplomacy if they are to resolve the legitimate but conflicting demands made by directors, choreographers, scenographers and technicians. Almost every lighting design involves some degree of pragmatic compromise based on assessing conflicting priorities in a climate of financial stringency. All carried out within a corset of safety regulations.

The initial role of theatre consultants tended to be one of damage limitation, with the timing and terms of appointment often resulting in their influence being 'too little, too late'. But the new profession quickly established a major corporate role in theatre planning, now often appointed before the architect in order to research the feasibility of a theatre, advise on its format, and assist with preparation of the brief. Such responsibility, however, does make theatre consultants very vulnerable: an easily identifiable target for any shortcomings, real or imagined, in any aspect of a theatre building. It is interesting that most theatre consultants seem to bear this burden with less paranoia than do many architects. Presumably this is a result of the consultants growing up in a backstage environment where emotional agonies tend to be short-lived and only surface-deep.

The contribution of theatre consultancy has now become so integral to most projects that the only real way to become aware of its importance is to look at the shortcomings of theatres built without input from a consultancy practice. As a result, to proceed without a theatre consultant is now regarded as a courageous decision which is inevitably regretted – certainly by the user, if not always by the client.

But just what is this input? Essentially it is concerned both with a catalytic contribution to the creative debate about the whole philosophy of the building's design and with the detailed planning of all the features which are special to a theatre. Theatre consultancy involves philosophy, engineering and, perhaps most important, street knowledge of what actually happens in the daily life of a theatre. It needs a team of open-minded specialists who have available to them a database of the scope that can only really be accumulated within a practice with a wide range of completed projects. Above all, it needs a staff who still return regularly to their roots for a bit of physical graft amid the nitty-gritty of mounting a show on an awkward stage.

The debate, both with the client and within the office, should be intense. Any creative debate is intense. A consultant's job is most certainly not to agree with the client for the sake of a quiet life. It is to stimulate all decision areas by ensuring that the client is aware of all available options and their implications. Proposals to the client will be formulated as a result of an internal office debating process between members of the team. That debate will be international: the concept of a theatre has become even more universal in a shrinking world. The decisions involve extended agonising.

Theatres for hearers

In 1790, when Richard Cumberland declared Drury Lane and Covent Garden to be 'henceforward theatres for spectators rather than playhouses for hearers', his concern arose from the enlarged dimensions. How would he have reacted to today's loudspeaker theatres? After all, the loudspeaker has returned our bigger theatres to a place for hearing actors more clearly than seeing them. I suspect he would have remained concerned with the effect of scale upon observation of 'moving brow and penetrating eye' with the result that 'the distant auditor might chance to catch the text but would not see the comment that was wont so exquisitely to elucidate the poet's meaning, and impress it on the hearer's heart'.

He would doubtless have taken pleasure in our rediscovery of smaller theatre forms where 'as the passions shift and are by turns reflected from the mirror of expressive countenance, nothing is lost'. And might he not also have welcomed the fine nuances of expressive countenance made visible by the cameras of film and video?

But how about our theatres of spectacle where voice is amplified to a degree that it no longer seems to be associated with a particular actor? It can look like mime, even when it is not. Composers of today's music theatre assume an electronic interface between actor and audience. This is not just a matter of the quality of the sound or of its total volume, but of a balance achieved by microphone mixing rather than orchestral scoring. The volume of sound is related to the expectation of an ear conditioned by amplification to a level which cannot be ignored. Electronic factors, culminating in the Personal Walkman, have influenced our expectations so that even opera can sound undernourished in a large house.

I am convinced that natural evolution is already responding to the ever-rising crescendo of ambient noise by developing irises for our ears. Perhaps zoom eyesight will follow. Then henceforward our theatres could be for both spectators and hearers.

The smell of success

The relationship between actor and audience has long been the major topic of any philosophical debate about theatre architecture. But a more technological approach suggests that we may have got it all wrong. It is not the proscenium arch that is the barrier: it is the air conditioning. Yes, in the pure climate of a modern theatre, we cannot love the actors because we cannot smell them. But relief is at hand. Modern science has not only isolated the magic pongs, called pheromones, but can synthesise them. A few squirts with an aerosol and you too can be a star. And surely these pheromones could do even more for that other important relationship: the one between individual members of the audience, giving them a corporate identity. Did all that bygone hygienic spraying of the auditorium with Jeyes Fluid ensure that the audience was less than the sum of its parts?

Painting the house

When I was lad, the buzzword was *reform*. Today it is *restore*. The reformation bandwagon was halted by our disenchantment with the new, while restoration was fostered by our guilt about our treatment of the old. Many new theatres failed to rise to our expectations because we had thrown the baby out with the bath water. It was an expensive lesson but we learned it, and most new theatres are now the result of analysing the old ones with a view to retaining the good features rather than just rejecting the bad. So the outlook for new theatres is considerably brighter in all respects except perhaps one: the lack of funds which favours patching up the old irrespective of architectural merit.

There are some aspects of the restoration scene that give considerable cause for disquiet. Before restoration became fashionable, it was possible to make reasonably pragmatic decisions about the compromises which are required to stage modern productions in buildings designed for an earlier technology. But do I detect a growing movement towards according a higher priority to authentic recreation of the auditorium as it was on its original opening night than to maximising its suitability for tonight's performance?

A crucial aspect is *light* and the problem is twofold. There are obvious difficulties posed by the intrusion of modern lighting equipment in a building with no provision to accommodate it discreetly. But with a good dialogue between conservationist and user it is possible to achieve a practical but discreet installation.

Perhaps more critical is the effect of the light levels of today in an auditorium of yesterday. The trickiest problem is the level of today's house and production lighting in relation to the colours of the auditorium decoration. Current fashion is to research the original colour by taking paint scrapings and confirming from contemporary press reports that the correct layer has been uncovered. But this original paint was chosen for the environmental conditions in the auditorium at the time of construction. All restored theatres come from the tobacco age and many of them also knew gas lighting. The smoke generated by tobacco and gas combustion produced a rapid darkening of the paint finishes. Light levels were so low that even in the days when houselights remained on during performances, an auditorium was much darker than with today's multiple light beams bouncing off the stage floor.

Are we approaching restoration in the right way? Should we strive to recreate exactly what the original decorators did? Or should we attempt to recreate the general spirt of the original intentions within the needs of today's performance conditions? Since safety and comfort considerations prevent an exact restoration of the past, should we not be more pragmatic in our response to the consequences of modern lighting?

Successful auditorium decoration is bright and exciting when you step over the threshold, interesting when you sit down and look around, then discreetly neutral when the performance starts. Great theatre architects like Matcham and Phipps understood this: surely we do them a disservice when we restore detail at the expense of spirit.

I welcome the interest of the art historians in the preservation of our theatre's architectural heritage. But I do have this uncomfortable suspicion that their subconscious priority is museum rather than performance. I do so hope that I am crying wolf.

3
Scenography and Technology

During our century, decor has undergone a gradual transformation into scenography. The word 'decor' tends to imply that the stage setting for a performance is in the nature of a background rather than an environment. But scenic structure, costume, furniture, light and sound have become so integrated that they endeavour not only to provide environmental support for the actors but also to offer a visual response to the text and music. The nature of this response has tended increasingly towards the metaphorical rather than the literal. The word 'scenography' implies that this integrated environment not only provides physical support and metaphorical comment but also determines the placing and flow of the action.

A performance can be mounted without the support of scenery or technology. But the simple planks and passion so beloved of the puritan theorists can soon dull the creative edge of a successful theatre company and bore their audience. This is hardly surprising since visual experience makes such a substantial contribution to live performance. Once the stage environment has acquired a scenic treatment, decorative or scenographic, some technology is required to provide physical support for the scenic structure and facilitate changes between scenes. Once the stage picture can be changed, it is inevitable that there will be a demand for the change to occur magically, within sight of the audience, for visual effect. Despite continuous proclamation of decadence by purists, spectacular effects have remained consistently high on audience wish-lists throughout the history of the stage.

Stage technology has never been primitive. Take away today's motor drives and computer controls and there is little fundamental difference from earlier centuries. Consider, for example, Drottningholm Court Theatre where the machinery of 1776 remained cocooned until 1924, requiring only renewal of the old ropes to function. The technology of that historic stage demonstrates basic aims which remain universal today:

- *Movement coordination* The carriages which slide six pairs of scenic wing flats horizontally on and off stage are linked by ropes and pulleys to one single capstan winch so that they move simultaneously. For hoisting vertically, an operating hand line rotates a large-circumference drum mounted on a shaft with smaller drums for winding the lines which raise and lower flown pieces. By using different sizes of drums for the lines, items of scenery can be flown simultaneously at different speeds.

- *Manpower conservation* Linking moving elements of scenery helps to minimise the number of technicians required to change the scene.

- *Mechanical advantage* Muscle power is conserved wherever possible by utilising pulleys.

- *Visual effect* A trap enables magic appearances from below, while a machine with parting clouds allows a god to be lowered from the heavens to resolve the plot.

The quality of eighteenth-century integrated movement, as demonstrated at Drottningholm, is so superb that it can be quite difficult to achieve on today's stage, even with the latest computer synchronisation.

At the beginning of the twentieth century, most stages were equipped with technology which was geared to the vertical and horizontal movement of flat, two-dimensional scenery in planes parallel to the front of the stage. Painted canvas could be hoisted up into the fly tower, lowered through traps and slots in the stage floor or slid off sideways into the wings. When seeking realism, as in 'box set' rooms with walls in positions other than parallel to the front of the stage, construction was by temporarily lacing together flat sections which could be stacked in the very limited storage space of 'scene docks' adjacent to the stage.

There were hints of new technologies. In 1896, Munich's Cuvilliestheater installed the first revolve in a Western theatre and, in 1875, Budapest Opera had hydraulically powered plungers to raise, lower, angle and rotate the sections of a modular stage floor. More universal was the replacement of wooden stage machinery with metal structures – a change accelerated by a concern for safety which swept across Europe after the catastrophic fire of 1881 in Vienna's Ring Theatre. But this had very little effect on the visual aspects of productions. On the great majority of stages the standard technology remained painted canvas, either as flown cloths or manhandled flat frames.

Designers had little option but to work within the conventions of this established technology. Pioneers such as Adolphe Appia and Edward Gordon Craig sought a more spatial approach but were prevented from realising many of their ideas. This was partly due to the limitations of available technology, especially for lighting, but was mostly a consequence of the entrenched attitudes of the theatre establishment.

In the earlier years of the century, conventional theatre tended to rely on a labour-intensive mixture of flying cloths and braced flattage. Most drama was played in box-shaped rooms of canvas-covered flats. Musicals tended to alternate between full-stage built sets and painted front cloths which enabled one full set to be struck and a different one set in the time required for the chorus to change costume. For more than half the century, many theatres remained 'hemp houses' using only muscle power to fly cloths and even heavy 'french flat' scenery. Counterweighting was confined to the major houses. Even in London's West End, the counterweight provision tended to be patchy with various sets of lines and weighting cradles left behind in assorted positions where they had been specially installed to meet the needs of various past productions. Mainstream musical and dramatic theatre aimed much less for the spectacular scene changes which had been pursued in the two previous centuries. Eighteenth-century scenes and machines had been dependent on low levels of candle and oil light for their magic, while the train wrecks and sinking ships of nineteenth-century melodrama were now the province of the cinema.

Many developments in stage technology were linked to new scene design styles made possible by advances in lighting equipment. In particular, the years between the two world wars were the era of the cyclorama. The cyc, as it became known, was born of a desire for a stage environment based on space and light rather than painted canvas. The traditional overhead masking borders, side wings and backcloth were replaced by a plain white or palest blue curved stretched cloth or plastered wall. In its most extreme form, the cyc became a permanent fixture so high that masking borders were not required. By curving around the sides of the stage, masking wings were also eliminated. In extreme cases, the top curved over the stage like a dome. The most advanced cloth cycs were suspended from a grid-level track which extended around the stage from one downstage corner to the other where they could be wound onto a vertical shaft. Under light this background became limitless space, treated as a realistic sky or as an abstract atmospheric environment. The sky option inevitably led staging style into its traditional pursuit of realistic effects. Many of the plaster cycs had tiny star lamps secreted within the plaster, and cloud projectors were developed to replicate any meteorological situation with such accuracy that all but the most dynamic actors were upstaged.

During the 1920s and 1930s, technological advances continued to respond to the twin requirements of handling scene changes and creating visual magic. Complex mechanical stages deploying elevators, revolves and wagons were being developed. In central Europe these were used for scene changing during intervals and for handling the daily changeovers between productions in the repertoire. Elsewhere, notably in New York's Radio City Music Hall of 1932, the machinery was used to create spectacular effects during performances. This was the live stage challenging the cinema on its home ground and winning. The conclusion of the movie was immediately followed by an overture played by a symphony orchestra rising on a pit elevator. The curtain – a magnificent affair contoured by thirteen motors – rose to reveal the 100-foot proscenium opening filled by the thirty-six ladies of the kick line in addition to the classical corps de ballet and choir, each thirty strong. Spectacular scenes came and went on elevators which incorporated a revolve. The orchestra platform could travel under or over the stage between the pit and the upstage elevator. To pay for all this required filling most of the 5882 seats for the four daily performances. The films have gone but the machinery is still in use.

There was a growing use of directional spotlighting to sculpt scenery and actors while controlling the focus of audience attention. But the light on the majority of the stages remained an overall colour wash, often with footlights producing an unnatural balance on faces and multiple rising shadows on scenery.

Throughout the inter-war years, most mainstream theatre carried on with the established scenic traditions. But elsewhere, particularly in central Europe, there was considerable exploration of new ways of defining and manipulating space. 'Isms' flourished. The appearance of labels such as expressionism, constructivism and selective realism was significant, not so much for the movements in themselves but as a manifestation of the new wave of creative debate that was questioning the purpose of theatre and the role of visual environment design in performance. Much of the experiment which developed out of this new philosophical approach to staging was motivated by spatial concerns. But there were also attempts to incorporate the new medium of film and adapt the techniques of photographic projection. These techniques were particularly useful for documentary comment at a time when an aggressively political stance was tending to replace the necessarily delicate subtext of earlier drama.

After the war, the methods of the experimental theatres gradually became the new orthodoxy. Design styles were now so subtle in their diversity that they could no longer be categorised into 'isms'. Any style became acceptable as long as it provided an environment which was relevant to the overall production concept of the director. Indeed, increasingly it became the scenographer who provided the stimulus for the staging concept, especially with directors whose approach to the text was based on literary analysis rather than visual response. Inevitably, this new freedom to seek an appropriate visual style for the stage environment was frequently overridden by two factors. One was the tendency of some directors to adopt a doctrinaire approach to their work. This might be socio-political or, more commonly, result from selective study of a guru such as Brecht who conveniently peppered his writings with one-liners which could be interpreted to give credibility to any doctrine. The other was fashion. There was an extended period when the scenographic response to nearly every dramatic text seemed to be the placing of minimum but significant objects on a raked platform within a high-walled masking box under an even blaze of white light. The natural grain of the wood might be stained and the metal tortured with corrosives, but paint was shunned to such an extent that some of its techniques were nearly lost. The art of scenic painting was restored to fashion in the nick of time.

Throughout the cycles of fashion, one feature which remained constant was the newly discovered importance of the stage floor. Although occasionally covered with a painted cloth, the usual practice over the centuries had been to leave the bare boards of the stage exposed. But there was a growing realisation that the floor was a key element in the acting environment, especially for audiences looking down from balconies. This led to it becoming a integral feature of the design, defining space and making a visual statement. Even if bare timber was the scenographic requirement, planks of the appropriate width and texture were laid, often to a format that was shaped and raked to make an appropriate space for the drama.

In the years following the Second World War, stage technology became even more polarised between the alternative needs of repertoire and run. The many new stages of Germany were specifically designed to handle the twice-daily rehearsal and performance changeovers of the massive scenery of the operatic repertoire. Most are variations on a standard format. The main stage area comprises several uniformly sized elevators extending the width of the proscenium opening and parallel to it. To the left, right and rear are wagons of similar area to the main stage. Any of these, carrying scenes, can be driven onto the main acting area. Dropping the elevators allows the wagons to lie flush with the main stage level. Soundproof shutters enable the off-stage parking spaces to be isolated from the acting area so that the scenery on the wagons can be changed while the performance continues.

There are several variations of the basic system. Some are a result of site restriction. The Vienna Staatsoper, for example, has no space for side-stages but wagons can be shunted to the rear or to understage for scenic assembly. In Munich a clockwise or anticlockwise rotation of wagons overcomes lack of space for a left side-stage. Other variations include degrees of sophistication in elevator design. These are frequently of the 'double-decker' variety, enabling scenes to be built within the elevator as well as on top. Some elevators can be adjusted to form angled floors – either cross-stage ramps or rakes ascending or descending from a plane parallel to the front of the stage.

Stages used for both drama and opera usually have additional elevator flexibility in the proscenium zone to make variable provision for orchestras. An adjustable proscenium opening is standard. The horizontal lighting bridges (often two- or three-decked) and the vertical lighting towers provide a moveable false proscenium, motorised to form any required height and width of opening. There is usually a turntable built into the rear wagon stage. This is intended as a production revolve, normally used during a performance to display various aspects of a single setting – the movement of the revolve often choreographed with actor movement. Such turntables have a diameter no wider than the proscenium opening.

As an alternative to the standard rolling wagon stage, a few German theatres have adopted a huge revolve with a diameter greater than the proscenium opening. The radius is then equivalent to a normal maximum setting depth and so the turntable can accommodate four complete scenes. Like the wagon stage, these settings can be for a single production or for several productions in the current performance and rehearsal repertoire. Such a jumbo revolve may incorporate a series of elevators and a smaller turntable for revolving elements within a scene.

Research has shown that certain optional features produce running economies that justify their capital outlay. For example, the provision of equalisers to lower the wagons to stage level in their off-stage parking docks has been shown to make a significant reduction in the labour required to handle heavy scenery on and off the wagons.

These big mechanised opera house stages are often criticised on the grounds that the magic is rarely apparent to the audience. But their importance lies in the way that they can be a cost-effective aid to running a heavy repertoire – both in saving money and in saving the time that money can rarely buy. To be truly cost-effective, there has to be a certain amount of design discipline and most theatres of this type have a 'bauprobe' or 'build rehearsal' where a design is set up roughly on stage using the levels and rakes of the stage machinery with substitute flats, rostra, cloths, furniture, etc. There are two benefits. Director and choreographer are able to check the practicality of the proposed space and minor adjustments enabling the use of stock items such as rostra may be suggested and demonstrated. Such changes, although not materially affecting the design concept, may provide considerable savings in both initial production costs and daily running costs. Moreover, it is usually easier for technical management to 'sell' this sort of idea to designers by practical demonstration than by discussion.

The machinery in repertoire houses can facilitate visual magic when required. But when spectacular productions are mounted on a stage intended for long runs, permanent machinery can be a hindrance. The final decades of the twentieth century have seen the emergence of international epic musicals which make a feature of exploiting technology for visual excitement. Apart from the basic flying system, the machinery used in these musicals is an intrinsic part of the design. The stage requirement is for a large acting area with ample clear off-stage space to the side and to the rear.

The century is ending with a truly scenographic approach to stage design. It has virtually become standard practice for the style and structure of each fresh interpretation for performance of a dramatic work to be derived from establishing the design of the stage environment both as a visual metaphor and as an action locator. Many styles happily co-exist, each one highlighting a different aspect of the many facets inherent in most texts or scores.

The doctrinaire approach to directing has become less in evidence. It has been replaced by a passion for deconstruction. In its gentlest form, a single element of subtext is elevated to provide an initial concept which often fails to be capable of standing up to a rigorous follow-through. Taking the pursuit of subtext to an occasional extreme, some productions have been based on the assumption that the author is writing from such a deeply subconscious motivation that the text is superficial manifestation of something completely different. If the audience is surprised, how about the writer?

In a scenographic era, technology has tended to become part of the production design rather than permanent venue equipment. Clear unencumbered space has become the essential floor-level requirement for virtually any stage intended for runs, long or short, rather than repertoire. Alas, avoidable encroachments on clear stage and wing space has been far too common until recently. The lead time to plan and build a theatre is so extended that the client's original personnel – particularly artistic direction and technical management – have frequently changed by the time the building is handed over. So the final users often have quite different ideas from those who contributed to the initial brief.

Technology for tomorrow's scenography

Is it possible to predict the likely direction of future developments in scenography? While it would be foolhardy to use the word 'probable', perhaps there a few 'possibles' that can be identified:

- Fashions will doubtless wax and wane, but the diversity of philosophies among theatre activists should ensure the co-existence of many styles from austere significant objects to lavish spectacles.

- The scenographic contribution of light could be poised for another leap forward. There would seem to be considerable unrealised potential in the new generation of instruments with internal microprocessors which control a fully dynamic range of the focus, colour and texture of the light beam.

- New technologies from other visual and performing arts media promise new freedoms of image generation. Perhaps this will stimulate another surge in the exploration of new materials, particularly those with translucent textures.

- Clear unencumbered stage space provides such fundamental flexibility that there would appear to be an unanswerable case for this to continue as a priority, particularly as repertoire programming is on the decline and unlikely to be sustainable, even in central Europe, if budgets continue to be subjected to the present tightening.

Poverty is often said to enhance creativity. Like all nonsense this contains some grain of truth. Certainly at the very heart of theatrical magic is the creation of so much from so little, rather than so little from so much.

Appia vision

Although directors are normally given the credit or blame for the concept of a production, the key originator of ideas is often the scenographer. Since most plays are about human relationships, most acting is rooted in naturalism: it is therefore the visual environment which can most readily effect the essential leap from reality that enables the deeper layers of the text to be explored. It is virtually impossible to achieve any true theatric magic without complex collaboration, and in this respect designers can be unlucky. The nature of a director's work with actors requires an extrovert determination which tends to ensure that they seek out and acquire design collaborators who suit their established directing style without challenging and extending it. Designers tend to be gentler creatures with the self-doubt that is inseparable from an artist's creativity, and they are less likely to sell themselves to the right directors even if they are able to recognise them.

Adolphe Appia never found an ideal collaborator. At least not during his life. However, his influence has been such that most directors, scenographers and lighting designers have become indebted to him to an extent that virtually amounts to posthumous collaboration. Appia's vision was ahead of the technology of his time. Who has the vision to set the challenge for tomorrow's technology? Or perhaps even fully exploit the technology of today? Is there an unrecognised Appia in our midst?

Green stages

What are the prospects for a more environmentally friendly theatre?

Unlike politicians for whom green is a relatively new bandwagon, theatre folks have an established green tradition – the stage's acting area has long been referred to as 'The Green' and references to Green Rooms go back to the seventeenth century. But now that a ban on smoking has cleared the air in our playhouses – although much of the tobacco in our lungs has been replaced by vapour from smoke guns – how can showbiz green-up its act?

With all government departments required to be environmentally conscious, cultural ministries will presumably make funding conditional upon a green strategy, even if the photocopying involved in producing, circulating and responding to this strategy is likely to use up another rainforest.

What are the green options? The United States Institute for Theatre Technology held a 'brainstorming session to produce a series of ways in which we can be more environmentally responsible while doing theatre'. This was no gentle manifestation of saloon bar culture, but a formal workshop billed as 'The Performing Arts and the Environment: A Philosophical Dilemma'.

Many of the resulting ideas are ones to which we generally subscribe already. After all, most of us are, at least theoretically, greens. When we fail our ideals, it is usually because we have been fighting the clock and we are subsequently consumed with guilt. And the measures we take to 'economise in the use of power and water' tend towards lip service rather than positive action. But many procedures that we would happily adopt would be costly to implement. Investing in 'hardware that is easier to salvage', and the 'time to salvage all such re-usable hardware', is not a serious option for production managers juggling with diminishing budgets. Neither does 'building in such a way as to reclaim raw materials' necessarily come cheaply. I have, however, fond memories of the legendary Jock Gough of Glyndebourne patiently straightening nails with a hammer. And in the same decade (the 1950s) I incurred Caryl Jenner's displeasure when I threw away gel offcuts rather than store them in the 'crackle-box' against some far-off day when we would do a play requiring the sound effect of roaring flames.

Who shall have the courage to suggest to one of our star designers that they should 'adjust expectations of audiences to accept and appreciate the use of stock scenery and costumes'? Some might even regard 'incorporate stock units in designs whenever possible' as a threat to artistic integrity, while 'use natural finishes wherever possible' and 'minimise repainting' represent the way we were rather than the way we seem to be going. Green intentions, like most aspects of theatre, are at the mercy of market forces. Nevertheless, it is interesting to note that economics have forced the world's opera houses into interchange of the scenery and costumes for complete productions.

Recycling is a clear goal. But while recycled paper may be fine for correspondence, most of it seems just too clinically wholesome for programmes. (Does recycled paper need to be quite so puritan or is it made like this for the gratification of our egos?) If we use recycled paper for what the USITT call 'administrative communications' are we likely to relax our vigilance and have even more memos and reports? Better to abandon paper, just talk to each other, keeping essential facts on disk.

I must admit to being a bit dubious about the wisdom of letting 'unwanted paint evaporate or add cement to harden it rather than pouring it down the sink'. And, although I am always happy to 'avoid the use of disposable cups for refreshments' I have met a lot of backstage china whose environmental friendliness was suspect, to say the least.

Urgent though it may be, the state of the environment induces, I suspect, a fairly low threshold of boredom. So there is a limit to the extent to which any theatre company can 'produce plays that raise awareness of environmental issues'. A greener backstage is not going to be easy. All the ways seem to need a lot of will. Perhaps we could start by agreeing to find the will to ensure that more scene designs are environmentally friendly towards actors so that they can walk comfortably, confident that they are not in danger from falling off or being struck down?

Trade fairing

Each year, from early spring to late autumn, a caravan of makers and sellers takes to the skies. With so many overlapping international trade fairs, airline timetables tend to supersede competitor's catalogues as bedtime reading for the captains of the stage technology industry.

To the cynical, a trade fair is a great opportunity for the sellers and their engineers to find out what their competitors are up to. Indeed, these fairs have been described as events where the manufacturers display their wares to help competitors develop me-too variants of the products, while the users amuse themselves by brushing aside all the good things each piece of equipment does and pointing out its shortcomings with ill-concealed glee. Whether the missing facility is something that anybody would ever need to use in a stage production is irrelevant: any market-oriented manufacturer will rush to do the decent thing and add an extra knob or two before the next trade fair. Without these exhibitions, much stage equipment might have far fewer of the kind of knobs which are only there because they are possible rather than useful.

But the fairs do fulfil a very serious purpose of giving prospective buyers a broad perspective on what is on offer so that they can establish which showrooms to visit for detailed discussion. Old hands soon develop a nose for seeking out the occasional new idea among the plethora of cosmetic tinkerings and software rewrites.

The rock and disco sections are predictably loud and smoky with stands awash with girls, long in the leg and short in the hem, to distract from the mindless gyrations of the lights. There is much talk of programmed design, but the effects tend to look as if they were originated by a random generator. Creative demonstration has always been a weakness of theatre equipment exhibitions.

Because of a generally recognised need for more user–maker interaction, plus cross-fertilisation between the various live and mechanical performance media, a considerable fringe circuit of chat shows has grown up around trade fairs. Attendance at these seminars can become a full-time occupation, rather like David Lodge's *Small World* where academics pursue enlightenment and each other in a sequence of round-the-world conferences. Such travel may seem romantic, but the reality can be escaping the bores rather than pursuing the charmers.

Once upon a time, the exhibitor's view of business was either gloom and doom or hallelujah: there was no middle way. But the organisers have now learned the art of hype. Get just one exhibitor to claim profitable business. Then, even when visitors seem thin on the ground, all the salespersons (they are the ones wearing ties) will claim that they are meeting quality customers. But a trade fair is rather like a theatre production: even if logic says that all the ingredients are right, it takes a drop of difficult-to-define magic to ensure a success. It is often the little things that count – for me it is big, really big, lettering on name badges so that I am spared the embarrassment of being unable to recall the names of familiar faces.

4
Funding

If funding were left to market forces, live performances would be limited in number and narrow in range. Many theatres which may appear to be commercially viable are sustained by such factors as philanthropic leaseholders and planning restrictions on redevelopment. Many performances are only possible because they are backed by 'angels' who invest from a love of theatre and its associated aura of glamour, or are attracted by a gamble where the probability of total loss is set against the possibility of very high return. Moreover, apart from the star names, most performers and their support teams provide a hidden subsidy by working for financial rewards considerably less than they might expect in comparison with other professions.

Until the middle of the twentieth century, British theatre had virtually no public subsidy. The only exception was opera which had some private support. But, by central European standards, there was, and still is, very little opera. The playhouses were built as speculative ventures and their economics depended upon securing reasonably full houses by following public taste rather than endeavouring to develop it. Consequently, a state of crisis has long been normal. There have been a few exceptions: the early eighteenth century, the late nineteenth and the early 1960s to late 1970s – perhaps three decades in 200 years when the talk was of openings rather than closures.

The 1960s and 1970s surge in Britain was unique. An idealism had been triggered during the war but temporarily inhibited by immediate post-war austerity. Suddenly it bloomed under an Arts Council which was benignly supported, at arm's length, by governments of both the left and right of centre. Britain began to catch up with the public service theatre traditions of central Europe where court theatres had developed into civic theatres supported by taxpayers who continued to regard the performing arts as central to a cultured civilisation.

Then, during the 1980s, materialism overtook idealism and so the century is ending with a theatre which is essentially dependent upon box office, eked out with sponsorship and some subsidy which, more and more, is dispensed in a spirit of charity.

Since the 1980s, corporate sponsorship has become an indispensable element in arts funding. Sponsorship's role in the marketing mix of a commercial business is concerned with image enhancement. The general aim is to associate the sponsor's product with quality and to emphasise the sponsoring company's caring role in the community. More specific benefits are the certainties of logo advertising, the possibilities of media publicity and the opportunities for corporate entertainment. Sponsors are not donating money: they are buying publicity.

The initiation of a national lottery has had a profound effect on British arts funding during the final decade of the century. In an attempt to ensure that lottery funds were not used to replace state funding, the Arts Council earmarked the new cash solely for capital projects. There was certainly a need for capital spending. Apart from some serious gaps in the arts building provision, the theatres of the post-war building boom had been so intensively used that they were now in urgent need of refurbishment. In an attempt to ensure local commitment and curb potential excesses of grandeur, lottery funding was limited to 75 per cent of capital cost. Inevitably this increased the strain on the limited private and corporate funds available for supporting performance costs. Regular announcements of multi-million-pound awards for capital development at a time of cuts in performance funding have made it even more difficult than usual for the public to understand arts finance.

With the majority of existing theatres in funding crisis and no foreseeable increase in national or regional subsidy, how would operational costs for all the new theatres be met? Projects seeking lottery capital were required to submit business plans showing how they would survive. Experienced theatre accountants had become too exhausted with the realities of today's survival to put a credible gloss on tomorrow's prospects. However, lottery grants for feasibility studies allowed business consultants to be hired to disguise the inevitability of mounting deficits with fresh jargon.

Funding now

As the century draws to a close, what sort of state is our theatre in? The view offered by the theatres themselves is consistent:

- Our productions have never been better, audiences love us and every box office is a hive of broken records.

- But, despite our hyperefficiency, we will close unless we get a lot more money very soon.

The first statement is an acknowledgement of the importance of image and the need to stress that funding problems are not a consequence of low performance quality. The second tends to be more of a threat than a promise. The proximity of insolvency is real enough but the theatre industry has demonstrated an almost infinite capacity for survival, even if that survival involves some of the loss of quality that has to be so fiercely denied.

These simultaneous statements are made with such regularity that most people don't really hear them any more. Of those forced to listen, the public purseholders find it easy to disbelieve and the potential sponsors are just confused. Our theatre industry which excels in communicating the finer points of human emotion and aspirations does seem to be rather incapable of either explaining its finances or putting its case for supplying an essential component of a civilised society.

It is not really a political matter. As far as the arts are concerned, we are back to consensus politics. The right were in power during the cutting but the new left are hardly vociferous with pledges to restore the cuts. The result is a financial climate that discourages risks to the point where imagination becomes seriously blunted and self-criticism erratic.

Today the post-war arts dream has turned a little sour. The spirit of the 1990s is encapsulated in the wording of an advert for an artistic director which set out in bold type such key phrases as 'work as part of a management team' and 'play a key role in the fund raising'. Below, in ordinary type, almost as an afterthought, came 'in considering applications, the Board will be looking for those with a track record in the international field of classical ballet'.

The way ahead

Since the heady days of the era that was known as 'post-war reconstruction' the British theatre industry has grown, Topsy-like, on the assumption that British citizens wished to move towards public arts provision on a scale hitherto only approached in some countries of central Europe. There was never any grand plan although there was a short period of euphoria. Funding has been mostly insufficient and always erratic. Despite this, the arts have flowered in post-war Britain. They even seemed to be flourishing at a level that could trigger hopes of a grand renaissance.

Neither government nor industry are likely to produce significant new money. Arts bureaucracy has expanded but rather than generate new money this has tended to absorb existing funds leaving even less available for performance. The civilising effects of culture are not much in evidence when it comes to the distribution of available funding. Each arts organisation, ostrich-like, continues to plead their own particular unique case for more. But if the government were to announce that every current request would be met in full, it is inevitable that the arts would be back in funding crisis within the year. The new funds would be absorbed, horizons raised, and righteous indignation would howl from every organisation whose revised deficit budgets were questioned. This is inevitable until we reach some sort of national and regional consensus as to the level of arts access which we are prepared to fund from national and regional resources. The yah-boo posturing of the political scene does not provide much of an atmosphere for rational debate. So, as a demonstration of the civilising influence claimed by the arts, it is up to those who believe in the importance of live performance to rise above the simplicities of a competitive philosophy. The arts have to learn to argue their case. Few theatre organisations have succeeded in selling an understanding of their budgeting problems to those who have some knowledge of theatre finance. So what hope can they have of getting sympathy from the taxpayer in the street or the minister in the Treasury?

Asking for more cake is not enough, although goodness knows it has to be done. The simple fact which nearly every funding client continually fails to acknowledge is that the cake is limited. My slice can only be bigger if your slice is smaller. When one theatre asks for more, they are in effect telling others that they should make do with less.

Sponsorship is here to stay and both parties to the deal need to make sure that not just the price but also the cost-effectiveness of the package is right. Sponsorship is a relatively new aspect of showbiz and there is a shortage of information on the deals being struck. We are told how much sponsorship cash is being raised but we rarely hear how much it costs in administration expenses to raise this sum and exactly what is being given in return.

Sponsors enjoy a buyer's market. They are courted by theatres anxious to close a deal. It is not just that theatres need the money in real cash terms but that success is increasingly measured by money-raising ability rather than by performance quality and audience satisfaction. Just how much do sponsors have our theatres over a barrel? Industry advertising budgets are high: just look at the corporate image spreads in colour supplements. There is some hard bargaining to be done: can we be sure that theatres are selling their 'quality-identity' at an economic rate?

Worries are often expressed about sponsors interfering with artistic policy. But perhaps their reliance on a contented audience and good press notices makes them less dangerous than the subtle pressures exerted by some public funding bodies seeking conformity with their particular artistic vision. Nevertheless, it is understandable, but a matter for concern, that most sponsors would prefer to be associated with events which are glamorous and fashionable.

Hospitality suites for corporate entertaining by sponsors are now regarded as an essential feature of every front-of-house. Is there just a chance that ordinary punters might feel alienated? That they might even feel a resentment that discourages them from buying tickets? We need the sponsors and they need us. Can we be sure that we are going about it in the right way so that short-term benefits will not be obtained at the expense of long-term paralysis? The pragmatic reality is that every good boy loves a sponsor and good boys do not rock the boat.

Public funding in the United States takes the form of encouraging private sponsors with generous tax breaks. This is only viable to any major extent in a nation with high levels of personal wealth, but it does allow taxpayers to set their own priorities.

The future may well be further cuts rather than just standstill. The focus is already shifting away from protests about lack of funding towards a search for more creative ways of spending what is available. Every theatre organisation is adamant that they are ultra-lean with not a drop of fat to lose. But survival may well depend on finding some way of pruning.

The funding authorities – national, regional and civic – will have a major part to play in making the pruning possible, because a significant hidden expense is the cost of public accountability. As taxpayers we all wish to see public expenditure subject to proper audit. But the complexities of the system for distributing arts funding has grown into a bureaucracy which dilutes the money to a point which makes a mockery of the cost-effective banners waved by the bureaucrats themselves. What is the cost of all the officials who process the money? And the cost of the committees, working parties, submissions, proposals, reports and responses? How much new writing could be funded by the phone and photocopy bills alone? As the cash has fallen, its availability has become ever more conditional upon meeting directives. Public accountability requires theatres to be seen to be seeking sponsorship. But what is the public cost of touting for such private money? Do the sponsorship receipts always cover the cost of the salaries, printing, telephones and photocopies used to get it?

Arts bureaucrats, realising that any measurement of performance quality involves too much sensitive subjective opinion, have created an assessment haze of plans, initiatives and allied hocus-pocus. There is a real danger that we could move further towards a situation where funding support depends rather more on what a theatre's administration is seen to be doing than on what is happening on its stage.

A simpler, more trusting approach to public accountability could release more money. But the theatres would have to adopt a tougher, leaner attitude to allocating expenditure. A fresh look at priorities. More people on the stage and fewer in the offices. Investment in the performances rather than their marketing. Audiences attracted by consistently high performance standards rather than marketing campaigns.

Might it sometimes be cheaper to leave seats empty than to market them? And has the pursuit of reality rather than illusion increased the costs of sets and costumes – not just in making but in transporting and handling? Perhaps it is time to rediscover the techniques of illusion which were formerly used to increase the impression of reality on the stage.

Faced with insufficient funds, a theatre can either reduce the number of its performances or lower its standards. Presumably theatres would prefer to maintain their production standards at all costs, even if this requires massive cut-backs in housekeeping and marketing which would infuriate the funding bodies who have become obsessed with measuring superficial manifestations of what they perceive to be good management. The alternative of reducing the number of performances has long been unmentionable in Britain although it is a strategy well established elsewhere in Europe. The case does not need to be argued for keeping theatres open all day and every day. We have all seen the catalytic effect that vibrant open theatres can have on the communities they serve. But all-year-round opening is by no means common around the world. Germany, Austria and Scandinavia are the only Western countries where you can be sure that public theatres, especially for opera and ballet, will be open every night for ten months of the year. But even in these countries, this concept is under threat from ever-tightening fiscal constraints. Will eastern Europe's highly subsidised repertoire theatre tradition survive the onset of democracy? In Italy, Greece and Spain most theatre activity is seasonal, while even in France and the

Netherlands there is a seasonal element. Spain is currently expanding arts provision: yet, in order to spread opportunity of access geographically, there is no automatic assumption that a theatre should be funded to open every night.

Each nation has to decide whether it wants to be in the big arts league. It is partly a question of whether the economy can afford it, but mostly a question of priorities.

Do we need a think-tank which considers and costs alternatives? Perhaps with a computer model which calculates the consequences on repertoire of casting and design decisions? Do we know the point at which it would be more effective to go strategically dark for a limited period rather than open for performance as a matter of principle? The prospect may be unpalatable but the debate should be held.

Funding is not the only concern for debate. Creative people are in danger of losing control of their stages. Could it be their own fault? In planning repertoire, do the performing arts always remember that they remain, as they were in earlier centuries, the public's humble servants?

An Ashcroft levy?

Throughout history, the most consistent source of arts subsidy has been the artists themselves. Today's writers, composers, painters and performers are protected from the levels of poverty that were commonplace in earlier societies. Nevertheless, unless an artist can command the commercial clout of stardom in one of the areas which are sufficiently fashionable to secure a profitable response to the pressures of market forces, the rewards rarely begin to approach comparability with parallel activities outside the arts. Low rewards and lack of security are often held to be compensated for by job satisfaction. But the agony that is central to an artist's creativity can surely only offer job satisfaction to a masochist. Most people working in the arts are driven by that intangible motivator called vocation — tempered, of course, by survival.

Many of yesterday's writers and composers still make their subsidy contribution through the saving of royalty payments on copyrights which have passed into the public domain. Paintings and manuscripts, frequently by artists who spent their lives on the threshold of survival, exchange ownership at ever-increasing prices. But the arts rarely profit.

Speaking at the opening of a 1987 design exhibition, Dame Peggy Ashcroft offered an elegant solution to the problem of increasing arts funding without recourse to additional subsidy or sponsorship. She suggested a transfer tax on the sale of all art whose copyright has entered the public domain. The auction figures for works of art, derived from competitive bidding, are relative rather than absolute. Such a tax would be unlikely to deter the buyers or sellers but it could sustain and develop the arts.

Let yesterday's art subsidise today's and thus provide a heritage for tomorrow.

Public accountability

In more cynical moments one is given to wonder how much of the national arts budget is devoted to funding the machinery of public accountability and the procedures of democracy. And what is the cost – in salaries, telephones and photocopies – of the protests that theatres make about their inadequate funding? How much of this expenditure is counterproductive?

There is strong pressure to seek sponsorship from the business community. Indeed public accountability now includes the necessity to be seen to be seeking sponsorship. But what is the public cost of touting for such money? Again, if salaries, telephones and photocopies are being costed, cynicism might feed a suspicion that they are being costed creatively. Cynicism might extend to querying the cost-effectiveness of that most sacred of cows – marketing. Any theatre seeking funding favour must be seen to have a high-profile marketing operation, even if it might be cheaper to have a few more empty seats.

How can we free theatres from the expensive apparatus of public accountability and the need to conform to the latest fashionable notions of the committees who hold the purse strings? Is there some way we can free entrepreneurs from the constraints of democracy?

5
Marketing

'Build your theatre on top of a mountain with no roads leading to it. Surround it with barbed wire, make everyone wear full evening dress, charge the earth and you'll be full.' There is more than a hint of truth in this John Christie joke. He put the spirit of it into practice at Glyndebourne and it worked. But it is certainly not to be proposed as a standard marketing formula! However, marketing is not an exact science with logical procedures which will ensure a full house. Marketing is full of the illogical gut reactions that are at the heart of the mystical art of performance.

There is a cynical definition of marketing which runs 'selling people something they do not need'. A more accurate and palatable definition might be 'selling people something that they did not realise they needed'.

The word 'marketing' came into theatre use during the 1970s as a label for something that has always been done in one form or another with varying degrees of commitment. The appearance of marketing staff, either as additional appointments or the redesignation of existing personnel, led to a more systematic approach involving a study of techniques used in other consumer industries and their experimental introduction towards gradual incorporation into theatre practice.

An insight into earlier attitudes is provided by the manual issued to theatre managers in 1933 by one of the provincial touring theatre chains. There are many pointers which are as true today as they have always been. But there is also more than a hint of the inflexibility of approach and stifling of possible initiative by the local manager on the spot that helped to run down the theatre chains.

There is a timeless truth in the statement 'As it is the company's business to please the public, the manager must pay particular attention to see that every member of the staff is polite.' The ways of ensuring this, however, have changed. Today's audiences would be positively alienated by a return to 1933. 'Men attendants should always stand to attention when spoken to by patrons. They must, when addressing patrons, salute and stand to attention. All attendents must always address patrons as 'Sir' or 'Madam' as the case may be.' Instant dismissal was the sanction against smoking, eating sweets or chewing gum and any lounging about or unnecessary talking was strictly forbidden. Equal opportunity? 'It is essential to engage girls smart, intelligent of good appearance. Middle-aged women cannot be engaged.' This extended to the 'Press Requirements' where the photograph entry is uncompromisingly cryptic. 'Plentiful supply. Non-copyright. Ladies preferred.'

But no theatre today has access to advertising sites which would justify anything approaching a print requisition of 25 eighteen sheets, 20 twelve sheets, 50 six sheets and 300 double crowns.

Typesetting costs were under scrutiny. There is a spirit of optimism in 'Managers will note that they should endeavour to delete any superfluous copy from the submitted copy of Daybill and Programme'. This optimism is recognised in the subsequent sentence 'It might be necessary to obtain touring manager's consent'. Contractual biographies may be a fairly recent addition to programmes, but the niceties of Billing are evergreen.

The advice on comps is still valid: 'Managers please remember that our seats are our only goods for sale, and the issue of complimentary permits must be carefully controlled. While it is necessary upon occasion to dress the house, the greatest care must be taken in doing so.' But surely no manager ever, anywhere, has needed to be formally instructed to 'Study the plans daily and note how things are shaping'!

The old methods of advertising shows and selling tickets lasted well into the second half of the twentieth century. Individual managers demonstrated varying degrees of promotional flair but most publicity continued with the same format and typography year after year. The ticket point of sale remained a small window which tended to make buyers feel that they had been granted a favour. One of the earlier marketing initiatives was the appointment of coach party booking organisers by the bigger touring theatres. But the most positive moves came in the late 1970s and early 1980s from the regional rep theatres which, under the umbrella of the Council of Regional Theatres (now incorporated into the Theatre Management Association), introduced training initiatives and published marketing manuals.

Marketing today

The starting point is what it has become fashionable to call a 'mission statement'. Its objectives inevitably start with *quality* and *accessibility*. (Exclusivity is an alternative possibility but unlikely to win friends in public sector funding in most current political climates.) Other priorities are likely to include *education* and *community outreach*. There is often an expression of commitment to the preservation, development and promotion of national, regional or civic cultural heritage.

With one key addition, the mission statement provides the basis for the desired image to be projected. The desire for *success* can only be implied in any tactful statement of objectives. But it is the primary element in the image of any performance organisation.

Image

Image is a key factor. The image has to (a) be identifiable and (b) convey success. Audience loyalty depends on their ability to identify with a theatre whose policies and attitudes are clearly defined and presented. And success can widen the range of public acceptance and approval – even from those who may view the expressed policies and attitudes with less than enthusiasm.

The power that a successful image exerts may be crucial. But achieving it can be very frustrating. A successful image is so intangible that there is no purely logical process to ensure it. The basis of success certainly stems from the quality of productions. Indeed quality is crucial. But it is only a start. Audiences need to be told by the media that a venue is successful. Told in a way that they are prepared to believe. This image of success must be conveyed with considerable subtlety if the message is to carry any credibility. While a certain amount of trumpet sounding is accepted and even expected, an excess can induce a counterproductive cynicism in the very people that the message is intended to impress.

The majority of the public do not understand theatre finance. They do not appreciate that, as a result of all sorts of possible accidents of funding, a theatre may be running a deficit yet operating successfully and cost-effectively. Their logic is simple. If the theatre is losing money, it must be because nobody goes. And if nobody goes, it must be because the shows are no good. It is therefore important to avoid regular horror stories of possible closure. Sooner or later there will be a crisis: but this crisis can be prepared for by an education programme. (It is fascinating that the performing arts, who are in the business of communication, are not at all good at explaining their own finances.) A subsidised or sponsored organisation never talks to the press about profit and loss. The financial position is a matter of operating surpluses and deficits. Financial success is operating within budget. This is coupled with an emphasis on audience size and, hopefully, audience growth.

Having established the desired image for a performance venue or a performing company, the sequence of marketing each production involves a four-part process:

- Getting the potential audience to know what the show is about

- Encouraging them to make a decision to see it

- Selling them the ticket

- Ensuring that the experience is one that they would wish to repeat.

In tandem with image, the other key marketing component is *Information*. A venue tries to match audience to production. The right audience for a particular performance will have two essential components:

- Those who have already experienced that particular type of music, play, dance or whatever – and know that they like it

- Those who have not experienced it but might enjoy the experience if given the opportunity.

A market-oriented arts organisation builds up a computer database with the capacity to identify the regular audience for each type of performance. Identification provides the possibility of targeting. However, if information is presented well, potential audiences will identify the performances as ones that clearly match their tastes. The challenge is to reach the people who are likely to enjoy a particular performance, if only they could be enticed into attending. The various classic ploys include placing difficult works in subscription series, two-for-one offers, and distributing discount vouchers at performances which attract audiences who are a potential crossover to a different but related type of production. Outreach and educational programmes have been developed by many theatres in an effort to integrate more closely with the community.

Publicity material to capture new audiences needs a high information content. It catches the eye and triggers a curiosity to look closer and read the details. Good posters catch the eye, even to the extent of crossing the road to read the details. Indeed my own personal assessment of publicity print is based on whether it might make me cross the road and, when I got close, whether it would give me the information I need.

Newspapers and magazines consist of acres of blank white paper needing to be filled with news. Radio and television are silent airspace waiting to be filled. Theatres need to inform readers and listeners. With the media looking for news and the theatres generating news there would appear to be some basis for a degree of mutual dependency. Alas, many newspaper editors and, to some extent, their readers rate failure as much bigger news than success.

Editorial coverage divides into news and reviews. A review is also news. If published the morning after the first night, a review is probably the most genuine news to emanate from a theatre in that it will inform about a new production faster than the word of mouth of the first-night audience. But the difference between a review and other news is the extent of control over it. Various presentation devices can be deployed in an attempt to manipulate treatment of news. But dealings with reviewers need to be conducted with respect for the ethics that surround the business of criticism, and indeed give it its credibility.

Performances need reviews. A bad review may not help fill seats but at least it keeps venue and performers' names before the public. And theatre can only proceed on the assumption that the next production is always going to be excellent. So there is never a need to discuss whether to invite reviewers. The question is how to make sure that they will come. The first essential is merely an aspect of the general need to make sure that a venue and its activities are considered to be an area of reader interest. The second is endeavouring to smooth the critic's progress by attention to some of the details that contribute to the user-friendliness of a venue as discussed in the next chapter.

Decision to attend

If the projection of image and display of information is successful, there should be a potential audience interested in the possibility of seeing the performance. Next, the idea of actually attending must be made to seem an attractive enough proposition for people to buy tickets. When the buying decision has been made, machinery is needed to sell the ticket and to account for the proceeds of that sale. Thus selling seats is a twofold operation:

- Encouraging the decision to buy

- Selling the ticket

Everyone loves a bargain. Indeed, in the atmosphere of today's selling techniques, everyone expects a bargain. Virtually all seats for the performing arts are a genuine bargain since their manufacturing costs are subsidised. However, the clamour of the marketplace has created an atmosphere in which any buyer feels inadequate if they have not beaten the system by paying less than the published 'regular' price. Indeed, the problem of discounting has become that anyone on a full-price ticket begins to wonder if they are the only one. This is a situation similar to the airlines where most full-fare passengers are likely to be those who are able to buy seats with their company shareholders' money rather than with their own.

Theatre has few such business travellers but in many other respects there are similarities between theatres and aircraft. There is nothing more unsaleable than an aircraft seat after take-off or a theatre seat after curtain-up. So it is not surprising that there is a similarity between airline and theatre marketing methods. The higher regular ticket price is for those whose lives are too flexible to buy an Apex flight or subscription series, yet not flexible enough to risk a standby.

Consequently, theatre marketing has become heavily involved in promotional offers based on discounting the regular published ticket price. Discounting needs to steer a delicate path between attracting audiences with apparent bargains and not discouraging them with complex conditions and procedures.

Selling the tickets

How easy is it to buy a ticket? I go to the box office. Do I get a smile? Working in a box office is not easy. Many people seem to behave a touch irrationally when they approach a box office, waving their arms and showing signs of minor aggression when they discover that their favourite seat was sold three weeks ago. But ticket-selling staff, whether in person or on the telephone, are usually an audience's first personal contact with a venue. So the friendliness of their welcome and helpfulness of their attitude is essential. Fax booking has required the acquisition of new communication skills by box-office staff and the Internet looks set to revolutionise our buying habits in all areas.

Marketing tomorrow

Many organisations pride themselves on being market-oriented. This usually means that they only make what the customer has been discovered by market research to want. Design then incorporates the lowest common-denominator requirements of the 'market sector' that is 'target' for the product.

This approach seems inappropriate for a product which is connected in any way, however tenuous, with the process of education. Nevertheless, however lofty an arts organisation's aims may be, there is always some necessity to take market requirements into account – and to research that market by some process however informal or primitive – because no performance is complete until it has communicated with an audience.

Arts marketing research has tended to be conducted in very general terms, with effort concentrated on collection of attendance statistics. Information on broad categories of preference has been sought, but there has been little attempt to try to analyse detailed reactions to a particular production. The interpretation of operatic and dramatic texts for performance is becoming increasingly subjective. Perhaps it would be interesting to research an audience's understanding of, and reaction to, selected interpretations. But perhaps the current passion for deconstructing writers is but a passing fashion. Dramatists may soon be accorded the respect that has been such a feature of the treatment of composers during the latter part of the twentieth century.

The prime challenge in the years ahead will be to ensure that productions do not become market-driven and that marketing remains a servicing role which helps a performance to find its audience. One thing seems certain: marketing is unlikely to become an exact science and will continue to depend on creative instincts rather than on mere logical procedures.

Flying stalls

An eminent consultant was at work with his steel rule. Not in the rarefied atmosphere of the consulting room, but while visiting a client with a seat problem. The consultant was tall and thin, so the seat measurement being taken was not the width between arms but the distance back to back between rows. The phrase on his lips was from the airline industry: *seat pitch*.

And why not? There are strong affinities between aircraft and theatres. Both frequently fly with empty seats. There is nothing more unsaleable than an aircraft seat after take-off or a theatre seat after curtain-up. So, not surprisingly, there is some similarity between theatre and airline marketing methods.

At the show or in the air, it is unlikely that the person in the next seat has paid the same price. There is a high no-strings charge for the few whose lives are too flexible for an Apex fare or subscription ticket, but not flexible enough for standby. New York and London have half-price ticket booths to unload surplus theatre seats. The airlines use bucket shops.

Theatre price differentials are based mainly on sightline. In the air they vary with seat comfort and service. How long before theatre seats divide into first, club and economy? Royal Irving with sleeperseats and champagne, Gracious Garrick with recliners and canapes, Theatric Tourist on benches with plonk from an understaffed bar (all the usherettes would be up-front with Irving and Garrick).

Well, at least theatre audiences can leave before the end without a parachute!

But, removing tongue from cheek, there is one area where theatre must surely always follow the airline's example: the maintenance of safety standards irrespective of the number of occupied seats.

6
The User-friendly Theatre

The performing arts are a people industry involving artists and audience in an exploration of human emotions, aspirations and interactions.

A theatre must provide a sympathetic environment for performers to communicate the ideas and visions of creative teams of writers, composers, choreographers, scenographers and technicians. This interaction of performers and audience is fragile. It needs to be nourished and cared for.

How can we ensure that we provide an environment in which artists enjoy performing and audience enjoy attending? Apart from improving the quality of performance, contented artists are more likely to be prepared to accept lower fees and contented audiences higher ticket prices.

Some arts venues are a pleasure to visit as audience. Some are a pleasure to perform in. A few are neither. Fortunately, many are both. But it is something that has to be worked at.

The audience

User-friendliness starts with marketing. But the process which results in buying a ticket is only the very beginning.

When we arrive, does the building seem to vibrate in a spirit of come hither? Many modern theatres have glass walls: does the interior glow with welcome? Warm in winter and cool in summer?

As we go through the door, is a member of the house management team immediately visible and easily identifiable? If we look a little bit lost, does that person say 'Hello!' and offer help. But hopefully the signposting is good and audience circulation paths so clear that where to go is obvious.

How user-friendly are the cloakrooms? A coat peg for everyone? Enough attendants or an easy-to-understand do-it-yourself system? Free? No charge: after paying a sizeable sum for a ticket, any surcharges, however small, are an irritation. I hope the programmes are free. In European theatres and concert halls a feature which can really make the user feel used is the need to buy programmes from an usher who is fiddling with change and consequently too busy to welcome people and help them find their seats. In Paris, usherettes even expect a tip for showing you to a seat for which you have already paid a ransom. Most of Asia has followed the North American practice of free programmes. Europe should follow.

Are the foyers buzzing with activity? One of the most exciting developments of recent years has been the open-all-day concept. How well it works is dependent upon how centrally situated the building is. In the shopping or business centre of a city, a theatre can become a natural meeting place. And pre-performance live music can get the audience into the right anticipatory mood. But it must be live: no recordings.

Time to enter the auditorium. It should be an exciting moment. If the architect has done a good job, we will feel that we are entering an important place. Perhaps this thrill of anticipation will be triggered by the magic of elegant decorations, lush seating, warm colours and possibly some gilding. Alternatively, it could be just the mystery of a darkly neutral box. Perhaps it is because I am old but I love the stage to be hidden behind a curtain glowing with a soft light. What is behind it? Hold back, reveal the excitement carefully. Many drama directors like the stage and its scenery to be exposed to the audience as soon as they enter. If so, please make it dark and mysterious.

By now the house staff are probably having some trouble in getting the stragglers into the auditorium. Hopefully everyone has seen the polite notices requesting silenced digital watches and cellphones. As I am offering personal preferences, let me say that I like a mellow but insistent tone to advise me to take my seat. In theory voice announcements provide a human touch but the reality is usually close to verbal graffiti. All these 'ladies and gentlemen, the performance will commence in 3 minutes, 2 minutes, 1 minute, the curtain is about to rise' announcements sound too much like an airport or railway station. When there is just a tone, it is often the standard $A = 440$ concert pitch to which orchestras tune. Great. But remember to adjust the tone for a performance with period instruments played at a lower pitch.

A user-friendly arts centre does not, of course, admit latecomers. But it has large high-quality video monitors to relay the stage action to those who, inevitably, got caught in traffic. And if anyone has to leave the auditorium, the ushers stationed inside will help with opening the exit doors to avoid noise. Hopefully the architect has provided adequate light-traps to exclude light when these doors are opened.

Regulars will know how to find their seats. Others may need help – smiling help. Is the numbering really clear?

If considerably less than full, the house may have to be 'dressed' by strategic spacing of the audience to give an impression that there appear to be more people than there actually are. Perhaps even 'papering' with some complimentary seats.

In a user-friendly auditorium, individual members of the audience never feel isolated: they are aware of each other and the audience becomes so much more than the sum of its parts.

Surtitles are now standard for opera sung in an unfamiliar language. When projected at the top of the proscenium they can be distracting for those who do not wish help. At the Metropolitan Opera House in New York the titles are displayed on individual switched screens in each seat back. With the possibility of multilingual options, this technology will surely become indispensable for any opera house with aspirations to user-friendliness.

Once the show starts, house staff are very busy tidying up, replenishing leaflets and getting ready for the interval. They have to do it quietly because acoustic separation between foyer and auditorium is rarely total, particularly in older buildings.

With so many people to serve in such a short time, interval refreshments are a logistic nightmare which is not helped by people like me who never order in advance. Well, I can't predict what I will want to drink! But I do not mind the wait if the staff are cheerful. However, if you really do want to encourage me to order in advance, please do not pour the drinks too early. I like my gin with its ice unmelted and its tonic unopened to preserve the fizz.

Show over, time to go home. Sometimes I feel that the staff just cannot wait to get me out and shut the doors. Not, of course, the house management who will be standing with their backs to the exits in order to face the audience going out, smiling and saying good night to people who catch their eye. Any poster and publicity materials facing the audience on their way out will be advertising future performances that are likely to be of interest to this particular audience.

Dick Condon once said to me: 'I went to see a show last night. In the foyer there was a notice which said "no hot meals served after 7.30". Now surely everybody knows that such a notice should read "delicious hot meals available until 7.30".' A small point but a strong indicator of the attitude that drives a user-friendly front-of-house.

Everything should focus on ensuring that attending a performance is such a pleasant experience that the audience will want to return again and again.

Critics

There is one category of audience who should perhaps be accorded their own special variation of user-friendly treatment. They may be small in number and occasional in attendance, but powerful in influence. So it makes sense to smooth the critic's progress by attention to such details as:

- Invite in writing and follow-up by telephone.

- Establish whether tickets are to be sent or collected on arrival.

- Allocate good seats in the reviewer's preferred section of the house. Seats should be on a gangway – a fast getaway may be needed to meet a deadline. And in a small town the critic may be the duty reporter liable to be called to any fire big enough to upstage a first performance.

- Never seat critics together unless they have requested this.

- Critics cannot be influenced, but it does no harm if advance press information includes some kind critical quotes from earlier touring dates.

- Critics need an 'angle' to a notice. It is legitimate to 'feed' a local paper critic who is not particularly an arts enthusiast and whose review is just one of a whole series of bits of copy to be written against tonight's deadline. Local or personality angles can be dropped into telephone conversations. Or there may be a 'how the show nearly didn't go on'. (The curtain was embarrassingly delayed, and the audience a touch restive, at the start of an eminent actor's one-man-show. But a whispered 'he can't get his beard to stick' ensured that the review was treated by the subeditors as newsworthy of a banner headline in a prominent position on the leader page.)

- Welcome the critic in the foyer. Have a copy of the programme ready and ask about interval drink preference. Do not talk about the show.

- Make sure the interval drink is ready. Many critics like to be left alone to scribble or just think. However, a local paper's reviewer may also be the arts reporter and interested in talking about the next show or sounding out on such ongoing problems as deficits and the state of relations with Councillor Biggs. But never talk about the current performance except to answer questions.

- Make sure that the box office takes any calls and relays them immediately through the house manager.

- Make lines available for phoning copy if required.

- Never be upset if critics leave before the end – just be relieved that they cannot then morally write a really bad review.

- If, after any critics have left prematurely, an actor breaks a leg, the scenery falls over or the theatre burns down, telephone and let them know.

Backstage

Backstage user-friendliness is also mostly concerned with people. But there are a few obvious points of concern in the physical environment. These are mostly commonsense matters of health and safety, particularly cleanliness and an air-conditioning system which maintains a dust-free atmosphere for voices and an appropriate temperature for dancers whose muscles can be damaged by cold. The air conditioning should not, of course, create draughts which might cause scenic cloths and gauzes to ripple. Comfortable dressing rooms with adequate shower provision plus relaxation areas with refreshment facilities are an obvious requirement for people who spend most of their working day backstage.

Getting the physical environment right, however, is the easier part. At least the problems are tangible. More difficult is the understanding and handling of the agony and ecstasy of the performers and their supporting creative teams. The emotional state of artists tends to go up and down, instantly switching from a high to a low and back again to a high. There is a lot of idealism, and the pursuit of quality against the clock can lead to moments of near-paranoia in all theatre workers.

My own method of coping with temperamental ups and downs, learned when I was a stage manager, is to listen sympathetically but keep cool. My silent motto is 'don't panic' because I know that most creative tensions go as fast as they come. And the ups and downs of tension are not just for the performers who appear on stage or play in the orchestra pit. The best technicians are creative technicians, not just responding to requests and instructions but contributing ideas. Good follow-spot operators are in tune with the actor they are following. Like an orchestra conductor, they anticipate, leading rather than following. The sensitive flyman pulling on a rope is sympathetic to the phrasing of the music.

Caring technicians have an obsessive pursuit of quality of their own speciality. But working in the arts involves a lot of pragmatism. The process of selecting priorities inevitably means that some ideals get compromised. This leads to frustration and more of that rapid alternation between feel-good and feel-bad. Technicians are certainly not immune to the ups and downs of agony and ecstasy.

Backstage cynicism is often brought about by perception of what appears to be insensitive and unappreciative management. Managements are rarely insensitive or unappreciative – it just sometimes seems that way. The solution, inevitably, is *communication*. Fundamental to any successful management chain is the development of interpersonal communication through mutual understanding of job functions and related stresses.

In most of the user-friendly theatres I have worked in, I have observed that the boss walks around the building at least once a day with a smile or encouraging word for everyone, sometimes pausing for a question or a short discussion. I have myself tried to carry this into practice, not just when working in theatre but also when involved in theatre education.

There are some differences corresponding to the main divisions of any backstage operation – producing and receiving. In a venue which manufactures its own productions – with its own actors, musicians, technicians and workshops – the need is to foster a family spirit. Again, the key is communication. Performers and technicians are inherently committed. It is a consequence of their choice of profession. So they need to be kept informed, have the problems explained to them, their advice and cooperation sought. Matters should never reach the point which they did in one eminent British drama company a few years ago. The actors were having difficulty in getting a meeting with their rather invisible artistic director. At that time, there was a television programme called *Jim'll Fix It*. In this programme children wrote to Jimmy Saville asking him to arrange for them to do things like fly Concorde, go in a submarine, meet a pop star or a prime minister, etc. So the actors wrote to Jim and asked him to fix a meeting with their artistic director!

As a visiting designer taking productions into a theatre, I have found that the quality of the welcome and advance preparation can vary considerably. And I have observed the tremendous difference that can be made by a good advance dialogue about requirements. In most user-friendly venues a member of the top management team, usually the boss, appears for a few moments to say hello during the first couple of hours.

When I managed a receiving theatre, I visited all the dressing rooms 40 minutes before the first performance of each incoming tour, welcoming the actors, giving them a programme and inviting them to have a drink in the theatre bar after the performance. (I did not, of course, intrude during the vital 30 minutes when they prepare themselves to perform.)

Touring shows need to be made to feel part of the operation while they are in residence. The problem, and it is a considerable one, is to break down any feelings of *us* and *them*.

I am convinced that all of us who work in the field of performance have to acquire a knowledge of everybody else's job functions and an understanding of related stresses. This is a two-way process. It is not just a matter of managers understanding what performers, designers and technicians do. It also involves the performers and their support team gaining more understanding of arts policy, funding, management problems, techniques – and, yes, tensions.

I know that the quality of my own work tends to improve when I am in a user-friendly theatre. And I have been known to accept smaller fees. When I am in the audience at a user-friendly venue, my pleasure is heightened and the performance seems better than it probably is. And I am prepared to pay more!

The audience is the reason for a performance. They must be our prime focus. My personal passion is the operas of Handel. But I also love the Broadway musical and I believe that what we have to offer our audiences is encapsulated in a lyric from Ebb and Kander's *Chicago* . . . .

Ebb and Kander do not ignore quality . . . .

Give them a show that so splendiferous
Row after row will grow vociferous.

But they revel in the intangible . . . .

Give them the old razzle dazzle
Razzle dazzle them
Give them an act with lots of flash in it
And the reaction will be passionate
Give 'em the old hocus pocus
Bead and feather 'em
How can they see with sequins in their eyes?

It is our job to razzle dazzle 'em with the quality of the performance. But that is easier if we also razzle dazzle 'em with our friendliness.

Moving the rope

Have I just been unlucky, or do I detect a trend towards a loss of the skill to dress the house so that it looks fuller than it actually is? I have been in several audiences recently when I might have had some questions for my box-office staff if I had been the theatre manager. And I would certainly have had some hard words for the theatre manager if I had been producer, investor, author, director or actor.

On the worst occasion I sat in row P, with seat occupation solid from the row in front of me to the back wall of the stalls. In front of us were perhaps about thirty people in total, grouped in isolated pockets. I understand that the situation upstairs was similar. In allowing this empty acre between stage and audience, the management were surely demonstrating disrespect for both their actors and their patrons. Fortunately it was an excellent performance: we can only guess how much better it might have been if we audience had made closer contact with the stage. The management were the losers: we all told our friends about the empty house and how the frosty-faced house management had got their polite but humourless staff to turn back those who tried to move up in the interval.

With a properly dressed house we would have never realised how small the audience was. Such dressing of the house was once universal and is still standard practice in well-managed theatres. A touring management with a percentage element in their contract are only likely to complain if full houses consistently sell for less than the projected capacity take. So presumably theatres which no longer dress the house are concerned that seating upgrades will breed irritation at the front and jealousy at the back. But the secret of successful upgrading, whether in aircraft or theatres, is that nobody knows.

In the old days, an unreserved house was easily dressed by moving the position of the dividing ropes between each price block of seating. Hence the expression *moving the rope*, still used by traditionalists when inspection of the plan reveals a booking pattern indicating that the house is not selling in the expected proportions. The experienced eyes of theatre managers and their box-office staff can spot trends very early on, and they develop an intuitive feel for the extent to which the rate of selling will compensate for an early pattern of expensive seats lagging cheaper ones. However reassignment of the seat rows at which prices change can take place up to quite a late point. Indeed one of the easiest times to do it is when selling on the door. Alas, if the house is selling really badly, there may not be enough people buying tickets on the door to make such creative selling viable.

The key to discreet upgrading lies in the box-office staff identifying customers who will keep quiet about their good fortune. This is not particularly difficult for box-office staff who, by the very nature of their profession, rapidly become experts in human nature. Indeed it is probably fair to say that many people demonstrate an exaggerated version of their personality when confronted by a box-office window: certainly, any tendency towards loud irrationality, bordering on rudeness, seems to become emphasised. Singles are usually a reliable upgrade category since they have not brought along a companion with whom they might chat indiscreetly. And outside tourist centres, a theatre gets to know the faces of its regulars.

Moving the rope in order to dress a house should have become easier with computerisation. For one thing, managers no longer need to go into their box offices to look at the plans. They do, however, need to visit regularly to get personal feedback from the staff who, through talking to the public, have their finger on the pulse of how and why the show is, or is not, selling. Computers can identify upgradable patrons. And they can be programmed to identify trends. They could also be programmed to take rope-moving action. But I hope not. Computers can only take logical action and theatre management is an art. Like all artists, a theatre manager has to make lots of illogical decisions based on intuition.

There is, of course, a simpler solution. Single-price seating automatically dresses the house on the basis of first come, first served. However, even with this system, most conventional theatres, unless they are built with plain side walls like a cinema, need two prices. Because a major part of the art of dressing a traditional house is to ensure that you get people into the side boxes, even if you have to pay them to sit there.

7

Training

Formal professional training for many of the jobs in the arts is relatively new. Musicians, dancers and singers require clearly identifiable skills which a traditional educational system is able to devise ways of teaching. However, an objective assessment of acting skills is rather more difficult. This is presumably the main reason, apart from the actor's rather late acquisition of respectability, why drama schools are more recent establishments than academies of music, ballet, architecture and fine art.

Scene and costume designer training did not start to become fully established until the mid-point of the twentieth century. Formal education for the various specialisms in the production team has been slowly coming into existence over the same period, concentrating at first on stage management and only recently getting underway to any significant extent in areas like lighting, wardrobe and technical management.

This is not to say that personnel were previously untrained: merely that traditional training was practical and informal. The structure was one of apprenticeship without formal indentures, with the onus being on recruits to learn by observation rather than expect to be taught.

There were two traditional routes to theatre management. A few people began as office juniors in the head offices of the theatre-owning chains and climbed a very informal ladder with several missing rungs. But most made a mid-career switch from stage management. This path, sometimes referred to as 'taking the walk through the pass door', had considerable logic at a time when the word 'theatre' still conveyed a clear image, both of the building and the performance in it. The theatre industry's management procedures were based on established customs and practices. Written contracts often confirmed this standard practice but rarely varied it. Until well into the 1960s, most theatre finance was a straightforward matter of trying to balance expenditure against box-office income. The building owners took 30–40 per cent of the box-office receipts to meet their costs, leaving 60–70 per cent to pay for the productions. Subsidy was rare and there were no arts policy quangos to issue directives and initiatives requiring responses and submissions. In the normal course of their work, stage managers acquired a comprehensive knowledge of how the system worked. Most had enough acting experience to allow them to assume a dignified presence and speak with well-articulated authority.

There is still considerable merit in recruiting managers from backstage although the complexities of theatre funding, particularly with regard to political policies and public accountability, now require a more formal educational programme. The traditional route is still possible but the main recruitment source has become specialist courses in arts management.

Although education to graduate standard has become the norm for most careers in theatre, degree programmes tend to provide a broadly based introduction to begin a career rather than a qualification to sustain it. The subjective nature of theatre quality judgements makes this inevitable. But the fragility of a stage career also makes it desirable. Transferable skills are vital in a profession for which so many study that only a small proportion are able to enjoy a rewarding career.

The way forward

How well is the established educational system likely to be able to meet the future needs of theatre? How appropriate is the traditional emphasis on pre-entry study? What should be the balance between developing a wide cultural background and training in specific skills?

All artists need a highly developed degree of sensitive awareness and imagination in addition to more tangible skills. For performing artists, many complex skills have to be acquired by prolonged intensive study from an early age. This is particularly so in the case of musicians and dancers. The theatre artists who contribute to a performance but do not appear on stage – the production teams, backstage crews, and administration in the front office – can leave the acquisition of practical skills until much later and even re-skill several times in the course of their careers. However, they do need to start with an instinctively creative imagination which will be continuously honed throughout life, not as a conscious career development move but as a result of an inherent passion for the arts.

Some people respond well to the verbal analysis of formal drama studies while others are more comfortable with an approach which tends towards responses that are instinctive or even emotional. The rather intangible nature of theatre would seem to favour a choice of routes and there must surely continue to be opportunity for self-educated people to be accepted for theatre employment without any requirement of graduation from a formal programme.

Most of those seeking a theatre career, however, will benefit from a general education with a strong arts content, perhaps even with an arts bias. But how far should this pre-career education be specifically directed towards theatre? Many of theatre's most creative people have come from the widest possible range of studies barely related, or even totally unrelated, to the arts. When recruiting from well-educated generalists, the need would seem to be the provision of short orientation pre-entry courses followed by in-service, block release, specialist training for those who have identified their personal areas of interest and demonstrated appropriate aptitude.

It is inevitable that some possible worries can be identified on the horizon. There is a growing – and correct – preoccupation with health and safety regulations. This could result in training courses which stress technology at the expense of theatricality. Safety regulations increasingly require certification of the competence of personnel. This is understandable and indeed highly desirable. However, there is a risk that the demand for certification might lead to course syllabi which include content that can be easily examined at the expense of content which is relevant. This is a basic hazard of all education in such subjective areas as the arts. The award of a qualification depends upon assessment and factual subjects are the ones which generate questions with a clear unequivocal answer, sometimes as simple as yes/no. This is not to suggest that courses are being constructed in such a way as makes them easy to mark. It is just that the danger exists and is best countered by awareness.

Another, perhaps slightly related, hazard is that the traditional methodology of tertiary education does not give much encouragement to original thinking. Academic study is preoccupied with the development of ideas by analysing the writings of established experts. Since the analysis is in verbal form, there is little encouragement for the development of visual and audio imagination. Words are a major part of dramatic performance but they are only the beginning. The visual environment with its light, music and ambient sound has, like the actors' movements, a quality which is lost in translation into words.

The development of a good idea in the theatre is frequently untraceable. It may be the result of information received, images absorbed, incidents observed or emotions experienced. Lying dormant in the subconscious, these both trigger the creative imagination and are triggered by it. The origins of ideas generated in this way defy logical analysis and are at the heart of each and every art form. Creative imagination cannot be taught, it can only be nurtured.

Perhaps management is the area which may need closest monitoring in future. We live in a world which increasingly believes that management is a self-contained skill that can be applied with equal success to theatres as to frozen-pizza factories. 'Well, why not?,' the argument runs, 'they are both consumer products!' But surely theatre managers are theatre people who work in management, rather than management people who work in theatre.

Theatre, like the Church, is now rarely spoken of as a vocation. But it remains a job which you really do have to believe in. Theatre personnel are itinerants who are sustained by commitment. 'Job for life' if not entirely an alien concept is certainly a dream with massive odds stacked against fulfil-ment. Consequently the educational need would seem to be a broadly based foundation followed by a series of re-skillings at intervals throughout life.

But with predictions that future generations will make several career changes in the course of a working life, this may become the educational pattern for society as a whole. In a reversal of the usual roles, it looks as if life, for once, may mirror the theatre.

Please put your daughters on our stage Mrs Worthington

Mrs Worthington was probably very relieved by Noel Coward's career advice. It was, after all, in line with the orthodoxy of its time. Her daughter's thespian ambitions would have found little support from schools, friends, guardians, clergy or agony aunts. Acting academies would have sniffed at her talents and humiliated her at their auditions. She might have persisted and she might have survived.

Persistence is still essential and survival is still possible. But attitudes have changed. The stage has become so respectable that the British government has joined the rest of Europe in allowing its theatre minister to share in national corporate decision-making at cabinet level. The media imply that fame can be instant: we all have a natural talent which only needs releasing by market forces.

The marketing starts early. Mrs Worthington encourages her daughter from an early age to watch television for an education in media-wise behaviour. By the time of her first theatre visit, Little Miss Worthington is ready to head the rush to get up on stage for the panto song sheet, armed with suitable repartee to whisper into the comedian's microphone in response to his 'are you courting?' gags. Playschool, dancing academy and perhaps an audition for a fish-finger commercial (pending a revival of *Annie*), encourage a belief in the stardom to come. The move towards parental choice in the education system opens new horizons for schools with a careers adviser who acknowledges the potential of talented daughters and understands the complexities of higher education drama opportunities.

In their own way, Noel Coward's cynical little ditties are as exquisitely crafted miniatures as Schubert's songs. What would he have made of our college marketing strategies designed to encourage Mrs Worthington to place her daughters in their pastoral care? The minds of future social historians will doubtless boggle at the frivolity with which the nation neglected to inform its youth of the odds stacked against them in selecting a career in the performing arts.

Depending on one's point of view, theatre education has become either the beneficiary or the victim of the numbers game that now motivates college survival. The pressure to teach more students with fewer resources has become intense. Colleges have no alternative but to expand place numbers to meet the preferences of students rather than the national needs of industry and commerce. Is this really what the economists intended when giving their blessing to market forces?

The performing arts have always been subject to an oversupply of personnel. It is sad, but nevertheless true, that the high quality of our arts is dependent to a considerable extent upon wastage. Creaming leaves a lot of skimmed milk behind. However, until a few years ago, anyone opting for a theatre career took a calculated risk. If success proved elusive, the alternative jobs might be less interesting but they did exist. Today's career decisions have to be made on the basis of succeed or bust.

Young people cannot and, in a free society should not, be stopped from embarking on studies for a theatre career. Indeed, the spirit of Noel Coward's advice to Mrs Worthington has gone so unheeded across the generations that there seems little point in discouragement. But positive encouragement is surely morally indefensible. As established courses expand and new ones appear, it does not require very advanced mathematical skills to project the spiralling increase in the number of acting, design and technical graduates joining the job hunt each year. Presumably the sums have been done. But are we using the resultant statistics to counsel hopefuls? Does every prospectus carry a prospects warning? Many hopes will inevitably end in tears and a certain amount of human wastage seems inevitable. But surely we owe it to our children to try to limit the damage through a risk-awareness programme.